Guns for Good Guys, Guns for Bad Guys

Gun Violence in America

by

Michael R. Weisser

(Mike the Gun Guy)

in collaboration with

William A. Weisser

Volume 1 of 4 Volumes: Guns in America

Published by:

TeeTee Press
Ware MA 01082

Cover design by Damonza

ISBN: 0615883990
ISBN-13: 978-0615883991

10 9 8 7 6 5 4 3 2 1

First Edition

To my wife, Carolyn Goldstein, M.D.
Whose exceptional medical skills have helped thousands of children.

OTHER BOOKS BY MICHAEL R. WEISSER

The Peasants of the Montes
Crime and Punishment in Early Modern Europe
A Brotherhood of Memory

CONTENTS

CHAPTER 1

WE DON'T NEED NO STINKIN' FACTS TO TALK ABOUT GUNS

(Apologies to John Huston)

Last year Mr. Larry Simmons walked into my shop to buy a gun. I don't have to worry about identifying him by name because he'll never read this book. Don't worry, Mr. Simmons isn't dead. He's blind, and I don't mean legally blind. I mean blind as in he can't see anything. Like nothing, get it? I knew he was blind because he had one of those canes that blind people use to keep them from bumping into things. And when I looked out the front window of my shop I could see his guide dog sitting in the car. He didn't drive to the shop, that chore was handled by Mrs. Simmons, who marched in right behind her husband, pointed to a 22 target pistol in the gun case and cheerily said, "We'll take that one."

While she filled out the paperwork Mr. Simmons played around with the gun. When she came to the place where someone had to sign, she stuck the pen in his hand, guided it to the signature space and said, "Okay honey, now go ahead and sign." I'll deal with the straw sale nonsense in Chapter 6—that's not the point of this story. What is the point is that as she gave me a Visa card and I ran it through my machine, I asked, "How's he going to shoot the gun?" And she brightly answered, "Oh, Larry shoots all the time. We go to the range, I stand behind him like this (she moved behind his shoulder to demonstrate), then I guide his arm until he's pointing at the target, and then I tell him to pull the trigger and fire the gun." And they both chuckled back and forth as they took the gun out to their car.

In the interest of full disclosure I should tell you that the license that you need to purchase a handgun in Massachusetts is also a license that allows you to carry a concealed handgun on your person. I'm not sure if Mr. Simmons actually walks around with a gun in his belt, but he can if he wants to. And if he does it's okay with me. Because the truth is that as long as Mr. Simmons doesn't pull his gun out and aim it at himself, he's no danger to anyone at all.

I'd like to think that at the age of 80-plus, having raised a nice family and led a good and decent life, that Mr. Simmons has earned the right to stand in front of a paper target and pull the trigger of his gun on his wife's command. Larry Simmons may be blind but he's no different from most gun owners; he really loves his guns. And the reason he loves them so much is that, like most gun owners, his guns are his hobby. And hobbyists put a lot of time, money and energy into whatever it is that they do to support their hobby.

This is something that the NRA really understands about gun owners. And this is going to be one of the themes of this book. This is also something that people who don't own guns simply can't comprehend, which is another theme of this book. Unfortunately, most of the people who want to "do something" about guns, aka gun control, don't own guns. Yea I know, this one used to belong to the NRA, and that one went out and got himself a carry-concealed permit. But Michael Bloomberg has never been in a gun shop. And when he talks about the need to make tougher gun laws, or make it more difficult to buy certain types of guns, the bad guys don't hear him but the NRA makes sure that the good guys do. And they don't like what they hear because, a la Larry Simmons, they're good guys and they don't need anyone telling them how to behave with their guns. And they also know that Michael Bloomberg has never been in a gun shop.

Don't get me wrong. This book isn't an apologia for the NRA, nor am I about to start waxing eloquent about all those poor, misunderstood gun owners from whom we can all learn so much about *real* American values. I always thought that we learn from going to school, and I've never been comfortable with the idea that good, old-fashioned "common sense" trumps hard facts. And when it comes to hard facts, the NRA and the pro-gun crowd either ignores or distorts the facts that don't support their point of view. Which I'm happy to say is also the case with the gun control crowd.

The reason I wrote this book is to ground the discussion about guns in some real facts and try to explain why the current pro-gun and anti-gun positions are so wide of the mark. I didn't dig up any new facts; between the data collected by the FBI, the BJS, the Census and the CDC, anyone can get their hands on the same information that I have used. What's different about this book is that I'm going to take the facts, do use some simple arithmetic and filter the results of my calculations through thirty-five years of hands-on experience in the gun business. Which is something that no other book about guns has done. Because if there was such a book out there, you wouldn't need to read this one.

When I talk about the gun business I mean the people who make, sell and own guns. I can't find a single person considered to be an opinion-maker in the national debate about guns who fits into any of those categories, and that's true for both sides of the argument. I'm not sure that Wayne LaPierre has ever actually shot a gun. I know that Michael Bloomberg hasn't. Which doesn't make what they say about guns wrong. It's just a very incomplete picture. I'm not going to use this book to tell you what we should *do* about guns. I'm going to tell you what you need to *know* about guns. Then what you decide you want to do about guns is your business. And if the gun business is finally put out of business, my gun shop will become a Starbucks.

I got into the gun business back in 1978. Why? Because I was bored teaching Western Civ to a bunch of snot-nosed college freshmen and I thought owning a gun shop would be fun. I had a friend where I lived whose father was Chief of the State Police, I figured the cops would all buy guns and I liked hanging around with cops anyway. They were as close as I could get to the criminals and I always found crime fascinating, or at least I found books about crime fascinating. Plus, the gun business wasn't so respectable, and with my fancy Ph.D. I still ended up in a backwater Southern town with a bunch of very respectable and boring colleagues. In other words, I had a belly-full of being respectable.

So I went into the gun business and over the last thirty-five years have been a wholesaler, importer, retailer and NRA-certified shooting instructor. I am responsible for more than 40,000 handguns, shotguns and rifles entering the consumer market, and have also taught gun safety and shooting to several thousand men, women and children. The name I often use on blogs and other publishing venues, "Mike the Gun Guy," may not be original, but it's the truth.

A couple of weeks after Sandy Hook, President Obama (whom I voted for—twice) announced with great fanfare that he wanted the Centers for Disease Control to reinstate their research efforts on gun violence, which were abandoned after the NRA put some pressure on a few senators and congressmen in 1996. Let me tell you something about that research: it'll be conducted by a bunch of well-meaning academics who don't know anything about guns. For that matter, the NRA-friendly researchers who publish papers proving we are safer with guns also don't know anything about guns.

The public debate (perhaps "public argument" would be better) breaks out every time a particularly dramatic misuse of guns like Sandy Hook takes place. Immediately a great hue and cry erupts about how to stop such events from happening. And just as immediately the battle lines are drawn between one side who believe that the existence of guns has nothing to do with people getting killed, and the other side who just as vociferously believe that more controls over firearms sales will make America a less violent and safer place.

The basic problem with the debate about guns, as opposed to debates about other public policy issues, is that the two sides have absolutely no idea what the other side is talking about. They're not arguing about different definitions, they're not just using different facts. The two sides exist in two very separate universes. And these universes don't meet at any point. The gap is total and absolute. If you own a gun you think about it one way; if you don't own a gun your views on "what to do about guns" reflect an entirely different point of view.

It's not like, for example, the argument over the deficit. Both sides agree that there's a deficit, and both sides agree that unless some way is found to control it, the results could be very serious or worse. So the deficit debate isn't about the existence of a deficit or even its potential effects. It's an argument over how to solve the problem. Should we spend less and cut taxes? Or should we spend more and raise tax rates? Maybe the two sides can't agree on which way to go, but at least they are talking about the same thing.

This use of a common language disappears when the debate about guns breaks out. Think about Sandy Hook.

The minute everyone recovered from the immediate shock and the requisite period of public silence had passed, the two camps that always argue about guns began to speak up. The gun control crowd, led by the President, put the issue in moral terms; we need to teach our children that violence is bad. The head of the NRA, Wayne LaPierre, said that the issue had nothing to do with morality; it was all about protecting school children with more guns. The more the two sides talked, the further apart they became. Manchin and Toomey wanted a few more background checks, LaPierre and the friends of the NRA were out to save America's soul. It wasn't a debate, it was a caricature.

Does the fact that neither side in the gun argument seems to be able to communicate with their opposites mean that when they try to justify their own positions they know how to distinguish facts from opinions? Or to put it in a somewhat less-polite way, is what either side says actually true? I'm going to show throughout this book that much of what passes for "facts" on both sides of the argument are notions assumed to be true simply because they get repeated again and again, so they *must* be true; or what often passes for proof of cause-and-effect in the gun debate is, at best, coincidence and often not even that. The world of public advocacy about guns is a world created by, and nurtured by, advocacy groups and opinion-makers. And nobody, or hardly anyone, ever lets facts stand in the way of opinions.

To begin, both sides seem to avoid stating the most obvious fact, namely, that small arms were invented and designed for one purpose and one purpose only: to kill living things. Today we may refer to hunting as a "sporting" activity, but small arms were a very efficient tool for supplementing the diet with meat. As for killing people, we use guns to do that in the United States more than 30,000 times every year. So let's begin at the beginning. Over the next few pages I'm going to connect the existence of this unique American industry to the fact that we are the only consumer-driven economy in which consumers have free access to a product whose only real use is to kill people, sometimes multiple people. The story begins in Springfield, Massachusetts, which happens to be near where I live.

Springfield Arsenal – undated.

The American small arms industry first started in 1777 when George Washington chose Springfield, Massachusetts, as the site of the first federal arsenal to produce muskets for the Continental Army. His choice of Springfield was due partially to its location on the Connecticut River, whose many fast-flowing tributaries were already giving life to mills and early manufacturing concerns powered by water and then steam. Additionally,

Massachusetts was the home state of Henry Knox, a close personal friend of Washington, who later became the Secretary of War in Washington's first Cabinet. The site was chosen in 1777 and the first Springfield muskets were delivered to the Continental Army in 1795. Production at the Springfield arsenal would later be supplemented by production at a second federal arsenal located at Harper's Ferry, Virginia, the site of John Brown's raid in 1859 that preceded the Civil War. Ironically, John Brown was a native of Springfield, but there is no record that he actually worked at the Arsenal. He seems to have spent most of his time going around town yakking about the abolitionist movement.

Because this book is a contribution to the debate on guns in the United States, I can't mention the Springfield Arsenal without noting the fact that its existence inspired one of the earliest anti-violence cultural statements in America, the *Arsenal at Springfield* lyric poem written by Henry Wadsworth Longfellow in 1843. Longfellow and his wife toured the Arsenal that summer, and she later told Longfellow's brother that the poet spent the entire time haranguing the tour guide that the money spent on arms would have been "better expended on building a fine library." Wadsworth thought that the stacks of muskets looked like the pipes of a large organ:

> *This is the Arsenal. From floor to ceiling,*
> *Like a huge organ, rise the burnished arms;*
> *But front their silent pipes no anthem pealing*
> *Startles the villages with strange alarms.*

Ah! what a sound will rise, how wild and dreary,
When the death-angel touches those swift keys
What loud lament and dismal Miserere
Will mingle with their awful symphonies

Longfellow's poem is a reminder that, from its beginnings, the American small arms industry created both a backlash against gun violence, as well as a cultural symbol of American technology, marketing techniques and industrial innovation. In 1846, a former Springfield Arsenal gunsmith named Samuel Colt bought a tract of land alongside the Connecticut River in Hartford, Connecticut, and soon began producing both long guns and revolvers. By the 1850's, Colt was selling his guns not only within the United States but also in Europe, and his unique "rampant Colt" logo was the first industrial design granted trademark status by the U.S. Patent Office. In the decades that followed, every consumer product manufacturer would copy Colt's marketing innovation and adorn their products with brand-specific designs and logos to heighten consumer appeal.

Back at the Springfield Arsenal, however, technological advancements had occurred that would make an even greater contribution to the national, and indeed, the world economy. Beginning in the decades before the

Civil War, manufacturing techniques at the Arsenal transitioned from the "English manufacturing system" to the "American manufacturing system," which basically meant the replacement of skilled machinists using hand-fashioned parts to semi-skilled labor using machine-produced, interchangeable parts. One of the early proponents of this system at Springfield was Eli Whitney, who utilized the concepts behind the American manufacturing system to invent the cotton gin. The American manufacturing system actually first emerged in the clock-making industry in Hartford, then was perfected in the 1820's by Colt in Hartford and by the Arsenal in Springfield. The system then spread to other factory and manufacturing centers in New England and then jumped across the Atlantic to displace the English manufacturing system both in Britain and on the Continent.

There would have been no industrial revolution without the technology of interchangeable parts first developed by gun companies located alongside the Connecticut River. In addition to modern manufacturing technologies, gun companies like Colt and later Smith & Wesson were the first consumer product companies to develop brand marketing, logos and product catalogs. The Industrial Revolution and the consequent consumer economy were the engines that not only propelled the United States into the forefront of the world's national economies, but were America's gifts to every other country that subsequently made the transition from agrarian to industrial society. These gifts were the handiwork of the American small arms industry.

After the Civil War, firearms technology took a great leap forward with the development of smokeless powder that allowed for a much wider range of calibers as well as the development of rapid-fire handguns and long guns. The latter products, in particular the lever-action rifles made by Henry and Winchester, were used throughout the Great Plains and Western states both for buffalo hunting and pacification of Native Americans. By the end of the nineteenth century, there probably was not a single homestead west of the Mississippi that didn't contain at least one Winchester repeating rifle or a Colt or Smith & Wesson rapid-fire handgun.

At the same time that former frontier zones were being transformed into homesteads, villages and towns, the port cities of both the East and West coasts were becoming large, urban centers whose populations were being augmented by scores of immigrants arriving daily to take advantage of the burgeoning American economy. One of the results of this tremendous population increase was that cities became centers not just of culture and sophistication (as opposed to the less-developed rural environment) but also became associated with crime and violence. The urban criminality at the end of the nineteenth and beginning of the twentieth centuries provoked, among other things, calls for the control of guns, with New York's Sullivan Law being the first of what became numerous gun control ordinances that appeared in various large cities.

The perception that urban criminality was rooted in street gangs and other social manifestations of the massive immigration in the last several decades of the nineteenth century may or may not have been true. Nevertheless, the early urban gun control laws were built on public acceptance of the idea that guns were for "bad guys," who would use them to commit crimes and become a threat to public safety. This perception was heightened with the violence that broke out coincident with Prohibition and the attempts by various urban criminal gangs, many of Italian extraction, to use guns to control bootlegging revenues and territories. At the same time, a majority of Americans living in former frontier zones could still remember hearing "cowboy and Indian" or "cavalry and Indian" stories from older relatives. A resident of Wyoming who was thirty years old in 1920, for example, would have been the son or daughter of someone who was alive on June 25, 1876—Custer's Last Stand, a massacre that was still being celebrated on Indian reservations as a great victory.

The point to note here is that guns were a part of American life because the country had frontier and sparsely settled rural zones until well into the twentieth century. But the pattern of gun ownership and gun controls was already reflecting the degree to which America was divided between what was becoming the most expansive and sophisticated urban society in the Western world, and what had been and remained its less-developed rural zones. What was seen in cities as an unnecessary and dangerous device used only by criminals to further their illegal and violent ways, was viewed in rural and less-organized communities as a useful or at least historical item that fit easily into the contours and patterns of daily life.

As guns were beginning to fade from the forefront of the consumer market, a new consumer product, again quintessentially American, began to appear. Like small arms, which were invented in Europe, automobiles powered by internal-combustion engines also appeared in Europe before they were manufactured in the United States. But within a few years following World War I, American automobile manufacturing not only dwarfed the rest of the world's automobile output, but the number of cars that we exported to other countries that were manufacturing cars almost exceeded the total number of cars made in those countries. In 1926, for example, America produced more than 4 million vehicles and exported more than 400,000 to France, Great Britain, Italy and Germany, which together manufactured a total of slightly more than 500,000 cars.

Beginning in the 1950's, more than 5 million cars were sold each year, a number which reached 8 million annually by the mid-60's. Truck sales, which were under one million in the early 60's, began to surge forward in the 70's, and actually began to exceed car sales by the end of the 90's. Although we do not have exact figures on gun sales until the early 1970's, it was probably the case that somewhere under one million guns entered the civilian market in the mid-60's, a figure which began to move upwards due to reactions to the ghetto riots that both preceded and accompanied the death of Martin Luther King, Jr., as well as a generalized fear of crime that grew out of the upsurge in drug use by returning Vietnam veterans.

By 2010, the total number of guns in circulation and the total number of cars and trucks in the U.S. fleet were roughly the same—somewhere between 250 and 300 million. Both numbers are somewhat inexact, in the case of guns because we have no way of knowing whether all the guns that enter the market each year remain in circulation or are broken or simply thrown away. The lack of accurate figures for automobile ownership stems from similar reasons, namely, our data is based on car registrations, not the actual use or existence of cars.

But while the total number of cars and guns is roughly similar, the geographic distribution is not. The per capita ownership of automobiles is roughly one car for every two US residents but ownership is fairly evenly spread throughout the United States, with less than 10 states showing per capita levels significantly above or below the national figure. On the other hand, in the case of guns, as much as 65% of all firearms in the United States can be found in the 16 states that comprised the old Confederacy and the border states, along with rural areas in the Midwest, and the per capita ownership of guns in these states is at least 30% higher than the national per capita figure. Even though there has been a rush to acquire more guns in the last few years, the gap in gun ownership that first emerged at the end of the 19th Century between frontier and rural America on the one hand, and urban America on the other is still very noticeable. This gap in ownership patterns is rarely mentioned in the public debate about guns, but it should not be ignored or discounted in terms of how it impacts and shapes the debate.

The revolution in manufacturing that created the automobile industry and drove the American economy into unparalleled levels of output and individual wealth was made possible because of assembly-line techniques that moved from the gun industry in Springfield to the auto industry in Detroit. The two quintessential American consumer products are thus joined by a shared history of technical and manufacturing innovation which flowed from the Springfield Arsenal to the River Rouge Ford plant. And while the histories of these two consumer products have moved on very different trajectories, they continue to share one common convergence: the number of people killed each year using both products is almost exactly the same.

In 2011, slightly more than 32,000 Americans died in highway fatalities and slightly less than 32,000 were shot to death. By 2014, preliminary data indicates that the number of shooting deaths may, for the first time, move slightly ahead of the number of Americans killed in auto and truck accidents. There are no other consumer products circulating in the market that account for even a small fraction of the immediate deaths caused by guns and cars. And yet, while we go to great lengths to diminish auto fatalities through driver education, safe car design, speed and alcohol-impaired enforcement and insurance incentives, we do almost nothing to respond to deaths and injuries caused by guns.

My favorite pistol – John Browning's P-35 masterpiece.

Let's take one example of America's reluctance to create safety standards for guns. It is generally accepted that minimal gun safety requires that guns should either be locked in such a way that they cannot be fired, or locked away in a container that prevents unauthorized use. Even though a federal law passed in 1994 requires all newly manufactured handguns to be equipped with a safety device, *Massachusetts is the only state in all 50 states that actually criminalizes gun owners who do not lock or lock away all their guns.* In other words, while 10 states require some, but not all guns to be accompanied by a gun lock when transferred from a dealer to a consumer, only one state actually cares whether the gun owner then installs the lock. No state, including Massachusetts, requires that a gun lock accompany the private transfer of a firearm.

How do we explain our willingness to continue to absorb 30,000 gun deaths and more than 70,000 gun injuries each year without seemingly being able to enact even the mildest laws to regulate unsafe use of firearms? It certainly cannot reflect the fear that such laws might result in a significant downturn in gun sales and thus negatively impact a major category of consumer spending. Being generous, the total annual GDP contribution of the gun industry is under $4 billion. Americans spend that much every fortnight on bottled water. The automobile industry, whose products also result in 31,000 annual fatalities, contributes more than $500 billion to the GDP; in other words, guns are worth $1/100^{th}$ of what cars are worth to the national economy and yet we rack up just as many deaths from guns as from cars! Is it rational to accept 31,000 deaths from the use of a consumer product whose existence supports a hobby?

It may not be rational but at least it is explicable when we examine the manner in which gun safety is debated and legislated, because the debate about gun safety is not between two sides who share any degree of equality in terms of financial resources, organizational memberships, media access or political alliances. The only real player in the debate is the National Rifle Association, which over the last twenty years has constructed an impermeable Maginot Line around the strategies and definitions of gun control, against which the other side transports its arguments into the battle as if riding on bicycles that have not one, but usually two flat tires.

The reason why such an inequality exists between pro-gun and anti-gun activists is primarily due to the types of events that spark the gun debate, and the behavior of the two sides when the issue of gun control falls away from public consciousness. Historically, efforts to place limits on the use and ownership of guns have only occurred when a high-profile shooting takes place; either the shooting of a public figure like John Lennon or Martin Luther King, or a politician like John F. Kennedy, Robert Kennedy or Ronald Reagan, or a mass shooting like Columbine or Sandy Hook. Not that high-profile shootings always provoke a debate, because the attempted assassination of Congresswoman Gabrielle Giffords did not spark any outcry for new gun regulations, nor did the massacre of more than 30 students at Virginia Tech in 2007. For that matter, the killing of 14 people in and around the University of Texas Tower in 1966 became the stuff of pop culture legend and made Kurt Russell, who played the shooter, a national movie star.

So it's not the case that every terrible gun tragedy has sparked a public debate about the safe use and ownership of guns. But when the debate does take place, the NRA becomes both the main participant and the referee who decides the rules, because it is the only player on the stage that pro actively organizes around gun issues all the time. Counting a membership of 4 to 5 million doesn't make the NRA the biggest dog in town by any means. The AARP claims nearly 40 million, and the AAA says its membership is more than 50 million. The size and revenue of the NRA is nothing to sneeze at, but what really makes them powerful is that the other side brings next to nothing to the table. The Brady Campaign, for example, claims 1 million members, but has a total national staff of less than 35 people. The other gun control groups are even smaller and the most recent entrant in the debate, Mayor Mike Bloomberg's *Mayors Against Gun Violence* doesn't have a grass-roots membership.

In addition to a continuous and intense loyalty campaign directed at members, the NRA has also pushed its lobbying and legislative activities into the arena where most gun regulation actually occurs, namely at the state and local levels. They mobilize their membership through the network of shooting and sportsmen's clubs, of which most states have at least 50 such organizations, and they also tap into retail chains and discount stores whose revenues are increasingly derived from gun sales. The major sporting-goods chain retailer, Cabela's, for example, provided bus transportation for NRA members who wanted to demonstrate outside the statehouse in Hartford, CT while the legislature was inside debating (and ultimately passing) a new gun control law. When was the last time you saw a sign-up table for the Brady Campaign in a shopping mall or any other public space?

The reason that the NRA can mobilize its membership so effectively and vociferously is because every NRA member shares at least one thing in common with every other member; namely, the ownership of guns. There is no other membership-funded group that is organized so effectively around the ownership of a single consumer commodity and, as I will discuss in detail in

Chapter 2, most NRA members have multiple guns stashed around the house. And since the NRA tends to attract the more active shooters, people who often define themselves in terms of shooting for recreation or hunting, telling them that they might lose their guns because of a gun control measure no matter how benignly designed, is a guarantee that the cavalry will turn out in force.

On the other hand, the population that backs gun control measures is only aroused when a horrific event involving a gun takes place, and by and large they don't own guns. So their support of gun control or safe gun use is always of the moment, always conditioned by a specific event or series of events, and, by definition, weak and short-lived. This is what tilts the playing field so much in favor of the NRA. The country continues to absorb the human cost of gun violence, and the shock troops that march into battle whenever the issue is raised only represent one side.

The playing field is also tilted in favor of the NRA because of two other factors: (1) The geographic distribution of gun ownership; and (2) the manner in which gun access and use is controlled at both the federal and state levels. Recall from above that 60% of America's guns can be found in 13 Confederate states, 3 border states and rural parts of the Midwest, which means that just about two-thirds of all U.S. firearms are owned by residents of Maryland, Virginia, West Virginia, North Carolina, South Carolina, Kentucky, Tennessee, Georgia, Florida, Alabama, Mississippi, Louisiana, Texas, Oklahoma, Missouri, Arkansas and the farm zones of

Pennsylvania, Ohio, Indiana, Illinois, Michigan and Iowa. Together this region holds roughly one-third of the U.S. population, but also contains more than two-thirds of America's gun owners and two-thirds of the membership of the NRA.

Generally speaking, most of these states tend to be more politically conservative. Some are bastions of right-wing Republicanism, others still retain active embodiments of the Bible Belt, and still other parts lag behind the rest of the country in terms of cultural and social sophistication. What I'm saying in a polite way, and if it pisses you off it pisses you off, is that Larry Bird, born and raised in rural Indiana, wasn't wrong when he used to refer to himself as a "hick from French Lick." Where these areas really demonstrate a basic unity of outlook is not just antipathy towards government regulation of guns, but antipathy towards government regulation of *any* kind. These are states, after all, where a majority of the population still recalls that racial integration was the handiwork of the "federal guv'mint;" where labor laws and labor unions are largely unknown, and where battles over resistance to a national health plan are still at their most intense.

So it's not very difficult in these places for the NRA to create and sustain the "bogeyman" of a national government trying to "ram" gun control down everyone's throats. But what really creates fertile soil for planting and nourishing the 2nd Amendment Liberty Tree is the fact that these same states have virtually no state or local gun control laws at all. None of the 16 Confederate or border states regulate private sales. Only one—North Carolina—

requires a permit process prior to handgun purchase, only one—Virginia—regulates any aspect of gun shows, and none of these states have any requirements to lock guns or lock guns away.

The situation in most Western states is probably more extreme in terms of the existence of a frontier, anti-government mentality. But while most Westerners own guns, or at least acknowledge without concern their legal existence, there simply aren't enough people living in the Western states for the gun manufacturers or their allies to actively cultivate a following for political or marketing purposes. Montana, for example, is one of only 3 states in which the per capita number of FBI background checks over the last fifteen years exceeded the total population, but the state just went over 1 million residents, hardly enough gun consumers to lead or sustain a national movement against gun control.

The second issue tilting the playing field towards the NRA involves the manner in which gun regulations are split between federal and local governments, and then split again between different agencies at the federal and state levels. Let's start with the Feds. The 2004 Brady Bill requires every federally licensed dealer to conduct a background check on every person to whom the dealer transfers a firearm, whether it's a new or used gun out of the dealer's inventory or a transfer between two individuals who want to create a paper trail for their transaction. On the latter issue, incidentally, there is no reliable way to estimate the number of private gun transactions that take place, and while the gun control folks love to throw around the idea that 40 percent of all gun sales go unrecorded, in Chapter 6 I'm going to give you some data that may come as a surprise. Relax, you only have another 4 ½ chapters to go.

When a dealer places a call to the NICS phone bank in West Virginia, the NICS examiner is an employee of the FBI. After the customer leaves the store with the gun, the paperwork created by the call to NICS can be examined by the ATF. If a customer purchases two or more handguns in a five-day period, an additional form is filled out and a copy is faxed or mailed to the ATF along with another copy that must be delivered to the dealer's CLEO (Chief Law Enforcement Officer; i.e., the Chief of the local Police Department). Do the ATF and FBI talk to each other about gun transactions? Rarely, if at all. Does the ATF talk to the local police department about the behavior of a local dealer? Rarely, if at all.

If you think there are gaps in the regulatory system at the federal level, at the state level there's no regulatory system at all. In order to receive a Federal Firearms License the application must be co-signed by the dealer's CLEO attesting to the fact that the dealer meets all necessary state and local requirements for being a firearms dealer. But most states have no requirements. My state, Massachusetts, which is the most gun-regulated of all the 50 states, still allows gun dealers to run their business out of their homes, whether the house is zoned as a commercial location or not. Most states, particularly Southern states, have no regulations governing home-based businesses: gun business or any other type of business. I have travelled through the South and purchased guns from dealers who kept their inventory in the garage attached to their home or in the trunk of the car parked in front of the garage. I bought a gun from a dealer in Tennessee whose inventory was neatly stacked in his van, along with the portable counter and signage that he used at the more than thirty gun shows he worked each year. "I can get set up for a show in less than thirty minutes," he proudly explained to me.

One point about gun shows needs to be explained. Note this: there is no legal definition of the term "gun show" that meets the test of any state or the federal government. A gun show is simply a public venue outside of a retail location where multiple individuals may be selling guns. Gun shows are no different in form or function from any other type of flea-market, and in many places guns are, in fact, sold at flea markets, or even on a table set up on the lawn of a family who decided to clean out the garage and put the crap out for sale. Are gun shows regulated differently from other lawn sales? Maybe yes, maybe no. Federally licensed dealers must conduct background checks wherever they sell guns, but this process regulates the transaction, not the venue where the transaction occurs.

There are approximately 51,000 federal firearms licenses currently active in the United States. Perhaps ten to fifteen percent of these licenses are used by dealers who operate real retail stores. The rest, for the most part, have no commercial address even though many of these dealers transact firearms on a regular basis. A large number, if not most dealers are NRA members, if only because they can purchase gun liability insurance through the NRA at a reduced rate. Why would any of them, particularly those operating in non-regulated environments, welcome more government regulation of firearms? When the NRA says it "speaks for gun owners," there's no doubt that the gun *dealers* of America certainly heed the NRA's clarion-call to help protect their constitutional rights.

At the enforcement level, the breakdown of federal-state-local relationships is even more intense. When a gun is grabbed by law enforcement during an arrest, a search, or at the scene of a crime, it is usually recorded as evidence and that's as far as it goes. Although the ATF maintains a national missing/stolen gun list, there is no requirement for any state or local police department to submit lost or felony guns to the list. Some departments do, some don't. Not even federal law enforcement agencies (FBI, ATF, Customs, Border, etc.) were required to submit guns to the list until President Obama issued an Executive Memorandum on January 14, 2013. Only 8 of the 50 states require residents to inform the police when they discover that a gun is missing or has been stolen. But again, the local department that receives the report is under no mandate to forward it to the ATF.

Most law enforcement agencies are small operations covering a local jurisdiction. In fact, more than 50% of the full-time sworn law enforcement officers in the United States work for agencies that have less than 100 cops. Those of you who live in big cities or metropolitan areas— New York, Los Angeles, Chicago, Houston—think of police departments as large, well-organized, hi-tech operations, but the reality of policing in most of the country is far different and much more primitive. Officers purchase their own uniforms through a catalog, they buy their gun and ammo at the local gun shop, the Chief gives them a shield and keys to a cruiser and off they go. If an officer in a small, medium-sized or even large city recovers a weapon that was used in a felony, he has no interest in reporting the gun to some federal bureaucracy located in God-knows-where. He wants to solve the crime and clear the case. Knowing who first bought the gun after it left the factory is the last thing on his mind.

Which brings us to consider the next piece in the gun puzzle, namely, the rather bizarre legal labyrinth that has been erected over the years in the name of understanding and controlling the sale and ownership of guns. The fact is that every gun that is used in the 11,000+ homicides, 800+ accidents, 19,000+ suicides and 70,000+ injuries, along with the who-knows-how-many gun assaults where the trigger is not pulled, all reflect either illegal, inappropriate or unfortunate use of guns by people who were considered as not being prone to that sort of behavior when the gun first entered the civilian market. Had the original purchaser been judged as being prone to such behavior based on their personal and legal histories, they would not have been allowed to purchase a gun in the first place. This is the law in all 50 states, and the next section of this chapter will attempt to explain why the law doesn't work.

In 1968, following the shootings of Martin Luther King, Jr. and Robert Kennedy, the Federal government finally passed the first national gun control bill since the "Valentine's Day Massacre" law in 1938 that controlled machine manufacture and sales to the general public. The 1968 law did three things: (1) it prohibited direct, mail-order sales of long guns to consumers; (2) it required the purchase of all new guns to go through federally licensed dealers; (3) it gave the ATF authority to enforce the new law by allowing for periodic visits to dealers to verify the movement of guns from delivery from the factory or wholesaler to delivery to a retail customer. The recordkeeping that the ATF could inspect consisted of two types: (1) an Acquisition and Disposition list (known as the A&D) where the dealer would record the identity of the factory, wholesaler or individual who sold him the gun; and (2) the identity of the customer to whom the gun was transferred out of his shop.

In addition to the A&D, the dealer had to maintain a second form known as the Firearms Transaction Record, or 4473, which contained the name and address of the person receiving the gun, along with some additional personal information (birth date, height, weight, citizenship, etc.). The form also contained specific information about the gun that was being transferred—manufacturer, type of weapon, caliber, serial number—and the dealer's identifying information; i.e., federal firearms license number, address, etc. Finally, the person receiving the gun had to answer a series of "Yes / No" questions about criminal behavior, including whether or not he was a felon, under indictment, a fugitive, and several other disqualifying characteristics. Over the years several additional disqualifiers were added to the form, including questions about domestic abuse and mental competency.

I bought my first handgun in 1956 when I was twelve years old. My great-uncle and I were driving up Highway 441 outside of Fort Lauderdale and we pulled the car over and began walking through a flea market which consisted of a bunch of swamp rats (humans, by the way) selling all the crap that people had dumped in the Glades which, in those days, came to within a couple of miles of the beach. At one point I walked past a card table where some old-timer was displaying a pile of junk, and my eye caught a Smith & Wesson revolver with a price tag of fifty bucks. I actually had that much money in my pocket so I asked the old man if he would sell me the gun and he didn't ask my age, he just wanted to know if I was a Florida resident. When I shook my head sideways he pointed at another guy standing at the next table and said, "Okay, you walk over there, hand that ol' boy the money and he'll hand you the gun." I guess there was some local or state law that required him to sell his gun to a state resident. Obviously there was no law covering minimum age!

The next time I purchased a gun was when I moved to South Carolina in 1976. I had attempted the previous year to purchase a gun in New Jersey but the Garden State required me to first apply for a state firearms purchase permit and I just never got around to it. When I walked into the gun shop the following year in South Carolina I had to verify my state residency by showing a driver's license and also had to fill out the 4473. But the dealer did not have to verify any of the information on the form except my address and age, both of which were listed on my driver's license. The reality is that there was no more validation of whether I really deserved to own a gun, based on my history and behavior, when I bought a gun in South Carolina in 1976 than when I bought a gun in Florida twenty years earlier when I was twelve years old. Note that New Jersey, a liberal, northern state, wouldn't allow me to arm myself (a favorite NRA phrase today) without first applying for permission to the police. In South Carolina the following year, even after the passage of the federal gun control act of 1968, nobody cared whether I deserved to own a gun or not.

The 1968 gun law was important in two respects. First, it put the ATF into the picture as the federal enforcement agency dealing with wholesale and retail gun commerce. The agency first appeared on the federal landscape in 1886 as a revenue division but started enforcing the collection of excise taxes on liquor after the Volstead Act was repealed in 1933. The agency's most famous agent was Eliot Ness. In 1942, the ATF (then called the ATU) was given responsibility for enforcing federal firearms laws and in the 1950's also became responsible for enforcing tax laws on tobacco. In 1968, the ATF became the enforcement arm to make sure that interstate and transfer procedures (A&D and Form 4473) were being carried out properly.

The second major result of the 1968 GCA was the development of the federal dealer licensing system known as the Federal Firearms License or FFL. The FFL was originally instituted as part of the 1938 federal gun law, but it remained largely a dead letter until 1968 when virtually anyone who wanted to sell, import, or manufacture firearms or ammunition commercially was required to apply for a license and pass a criminal check. The rationale for creating a national licensing system rested on the assumption that making every dealer subject to the same procedures and same enforcement would make it more difficult for guns to get into the wrong hands, because at the very least law enforcement would have a record of how every gun entered the market, even if there was no way of telling what happened to a gun after the initial sale. Furthermore, through its enforcement procedures, the ATF could identify dealers who were transferring guns without creating a proper paper trail, thus plugging gaps in the system that previously allowed virtually every manufactured or imported firearm to move into private ownership without any trace whatsoever.

The 1968 law resulted in a national regulatory system that covered dealers but had little to no impact on regulating gun owners. This was mitigated somewhat with the passage of the Brady Act in 1994, which required every transfer between dealers and consumers to be validated by a background check instantly conducted by the FBI. The system went completely operable in 1999, and since that time more than 170 million gun transactions have been reviewed and either approved or denied. Aside from the fact that the NICS check has not been extended to non-dealer sales, there are other gaps in the data that make it very difficult to consider that this system is actually playing a significant role in regulating guns. For example, since the data from the 4473 Form that is transmitted to NICS covers the identity of the individual receiving the gun, not the identity of the firearm itself, there is no way of knowing when any particular gun enters the market unless a gun is confiscated by the police who then initiate a trace through the ATF who ultimately must contact the dealer who transferred the gun to the customer in the first place. And since the NICS database does not contain the address of the transferee, other than the state of residence, there is no necessary veracity for the address listed on the 4473 Form and the place where the transferee now actually resides. The individual receiving the gun must show a government-issued ID at the time of transfer, but who knows whether the address is current or not? Here's a schema for how the whole process takes place:

Gun is picked up by cops; cops send manufacturer and serial number to ATF Tracing Center; ATF sends trace to manufacturer; manufacturer responds with name and address of wholesaler; ATF sends trace to wholesaler; wholesaler responds with name and address of retailer; ATF sends trace to retailer; retailer responds with name and address of customer; ATF sends name and address of customer to agency that requested search. A recent study published by the Bloomberg Center on Gun Violence claimed that there is a correlation between how long a gun was in the market and when it was used in a felony; i.e., as the length of time between first transfer and confiscation widens, the number of guns picked up in felonies goes down. In the 12 years that I have operated my gun shop, I have responded to approximately 50 ATF gun trace requests and less than 10% of those requests concerned transfers that had taken place within the previous four years. The average gap between when I sold a gun and when it became the subject of an ATF trace is 6 years. Research conducted by Gary Kleck confirms my experience on a wider scale.

Furthermore, the assumption that a successful trace may aid local law enforcement in solving a crime doesn't necessarily mean that there was any connection between the trace activity itself and the reason why the trace was initiated. For example, I received a call from a Florida resident who was being charged with having incorrectly filled out the state form that is used in Florida to register private sales. He asked me to check the gender of the original purchaser because he claimed that the police in his jurisdiction were incorrectly charging him with submitting erroneous information about the person from whom he acquired the gun. When I told him that the person who had purchased the gun from me was listed on the 4473 form as a female, he replied that he had listed her as a male on the Florida form because she had undergone a sex change operation in the eight years since she had first acquired and then moved to Florida with the gun!

The point of this little anecdote, which became something of the stuff of legend around my shop, was that the entire regulatory system that has been created by the Gun Control Act of 1968 and the Brady Law of 1994 is basically a paperwork patchwork that, in its present configuration, creates lots of work for employees of the ATF and the FBI, but has minimal impact on the regulation of individual behavior with a gun. The system is based on two separate national databases, one controlled by the ATF, the other by the FBI, and they are only joined together on a sporadic basis when a tedious and often incorrect search is initiated that requires eight separate communications involving five different entities that more often than not results in the receipt of information that is hopelessly out of date. According to the Census, the average American family moves every 5-6 years, which means that 90% of the trace requests that I answered would have sent the requisite law enforcement agency to the wrong home. Is it any wonder that many police departments don't bother to conduct traces at all?

At the street level the legal confusion as to how to enforce gun laws and regulations is no clearer than the fog that surrounds federal practices. Take, for example, the issue of "straw sales." Both the 1968 Gun Control Act, the 1994 Brady Law their various amendments created classes of individuals who could not purchase or own guns based on previous behavior. Under federal law, you cannot purchase or own a handgun until you are twenty-one years of age. Additionally, the GCA and Brady prohibit handgun ownership by individuals who, among other things, have been indicted or convicted for a felony punishable for more than a year in jail, are a fugitive, were dishonorably discharged from the armed forces, convicted of a domestic violence misdemeanor, renounced citizenship, have been "adjudicated" mentally defective or are an "unlawful user" of marijuana, narcotic drugs or any other controlled substance.

Taken together, the number of people who meet one of those criteria for not being able to purchase or own a gun must be substantial. In addition, there are lots of other people who simply don't want to be bothered to get a gun permit in states where pre-purchase permits are required, or who don't want their names and other identifiers brought to the attention of the FBI. Since only twelve states out of fifty place any state licensing requirements on private sales, residents in the other thirty-eight states can easily acquire a gun by simply buying one off the guy next door. And since only eight states require their residents to report missing or stolen guns, we really have no idea how many guns end up in the "wrong hands" because they were stolen, lost or simply sold by one person to another the way one would sell any other kind of personal property, lethal or not. I recently spoke with a woman, the secretary in a law firm, who told me she had bought a .357 magnum revolver from me a few years ago but no longer owned the gun because she bartered it away to a guy who did some carpentry work in her home. "He told me he had a gun license," she said.

Meanwhile virtually every politician, police chief and policy wonk who has weighed in on the current gun debate has proclaimed that one of the most important ways to keep guns out of the wrong hands and therefore reduce gun violence is to increase penalties and enforcement of straw sale laws. The way the law reads, however, makes it virtually impossible to enforce because it has to be proven that the person selling the gun knowingly sold it to someone who themselves were not permitted to purchase or own a firearm. "He told me he had a gun license," the legal secretary said to me. And if it turns out that he didn't really have a license, did she *knowingly* sell him a gun anyway? So much for the utility of "straw sales" laws. By the way, hold off deciding for yourself about whether more aggressive enforcement of straw sale violations would lead to less gun violence until you see what I say in Chapter 6 about the activities of the self-anointed Toughen Straw Sales Laws champion, aka Michael Bloomberg, Mayor of the City of New York.

The other favorite change in gun laws favored by both the most ardent champions of gun control as well as the equally vociferous supporters of an unfettered 2nd Amendment are the laws designed to curb "gun trafficking" both by dealers and individuals. In fact, one of the post-Sandy Hook gun bills that made it out of the Judiciary Committee created a new class of gun traffickers who direct gun trafficking networks (I guess they would be called "super gun traffickers") and would be punished by up to twenty-five years in federal penitentiaries. As opposed to straw sale laws that are aimed for the most part at consumers, gun trafficking laws are aimed at rogue dealers who, it is assumed, take a portion of their inventory out of the retail gun display and sell it out the back door to someone who then carries the weapons to eager and waiting customers in some (usually distant) location.

There is no question that many guns reported stolen are later confiscated or recovered in locations far removed from where the firearm theft took place. The only problem is that this is true of many items whose theft and resale becomes the stuff of criminal enterprise. The difference, of course, is that we don't have a national registry of stolen Rolex watches. For example, in June 2013, authorities in Savannah, GA announced indictments against 33 individuals for gun and drug trafficking. The same gang also was charged with the theft of multiple automobiles that were either re-sold in Georgia or were destined for shipment overseas. The initial report did not indicate where the more than 180 guns came from that were sold to undercover agents of the ATF over the previous several years. But it did note that the cars had all been stolen in New York City. What was the headline of the story? "Feds charge 33 in Georgia gun trafficking case."

I'm not saying there aren't some rogue gun dealers out there, nor should anyone be surprised to discover that items are usually stolen because they have a re-sale value with customers who can't or won't acquire the same item through a legal transaction. But even if every single one of the 80,000 felony homicides and woundings that occurred last year involved a gun that was trafficked from its original source to where it was used illegally, this would represent just one percent of the guns that entered the consumer market last year and about $1/400^{th}$ of all the guns floating around in private hands. Furthermore, the moment we hear about a gun that was involved in a felony in, let's say, Chicago, and we then learn that it was purchased in a gun shop in Baton Rouge, we immediately assume that some gun "trafficker" got his hands on the gun right after it was purchased and then sent it up to gun traffic heaven in the Windy City. But for all we know the original gun buyer may have then moved to Chicago and the gun was stolen or sold, or maybe it was stashed in a car that was carrying a family up to Chicago for a visit and the car disappeared. Or who knows what really happened?

Right around the time I opened my retail shop some handguns were stolen from my house. Actually, not from the house itself, but from a little shed next to the house where we stored all the crap that we couldn't bear to part with even though we never used any of it. I knew who stole the guns—it was a shithead friend of my stepdaughter's boyfriend—but the local cops screwed up the application for a search warrant so that was the end of that. Anyway, about six months later one of the guns was recovered in Louisville, KY. Believe me, the shithead who stole the gun from me didn't drive to Louisville. But the gun ended up there.

One of my favorite guns – bought it at the Colt factory in 1980.

In addition to a legal thicket that makes even a modest attempt to enforce firearms regulations a hopeless task, the gun industry is also shielded from civil litigation by a law known as the Protection of Lawful Commerce in Arms that was signed by President Bush in 2005. Basically this law shields gun manufacturers from class-action liability suits which started springing up in the 1990's after the government settled numerous liability suits brought by State Attorneys General against tobacco companies. But the difference between cigarettes and guns was that the tobacco companies had to buy their way out of litigation by making annual payments in perpetuity of roughly $10 billion to compensate states for increased Medicaid costs, whereas the gun manufacturers were not required to make any financial settlement at all. Gun manufacturers are still liable if an individual suffers damages because a gun malfunctions while it is under warranty. But guns are the only consumer product which enjoys this blanket immunity from civil prosecution. And let's not forget that guns are also the only consumer product whose existence is specifically mentioned and protected by the United States Constitution! How much more protected can you get?

I'll tell you how much more protected you can get. Guns not only enjoy a blanket and constitutionally protected immunity from legal challenges, they also cannot be regulated as a consumer product. This was the result of an amendment to the Consumer Product Safety Act in 1976 which specifically prohibited the Consumer Product Safety Commission from regulating guns or ammunition, a change in the law provoked by an attempt by anti-gun consumer advocates to use the Act to ban or restrict the sale of handgun ammunition. Many common consumer products do not fall under the purview of federal consumer protection usually because their design and safety features are regulated by other agencies, for example, the safety standards for automobiles developed and enforced by the Department of Transportation. Yet other consumer products that align with firearms, such as handheld power tools, are regulated by the CPSC. From 2002 through 2009 there were 34 electrocution deaths from consumers using power tools, a product category that must meet certain safety standards in order to be manufactured or sold in the United States. An average of 4 hand-tool deaths each year gets these products regulated for safety but 31,000 gun deaths and the product still goes unregulated. Are you serious?

The NRA is certainly aware of the unique protections afforded guns, since they fought successfully for all of them, but to read the daily emails sent out to their membership, you'd think that total confiscation and the disappearance of all privately owned firearms was just around the corner. Notwithstanding the fact that we all enjoy considering ourselves members of an oppressed minority (or perhaps several minorities), the NRA's message to its members boils down to the idea that if you own guns your ownership is always at risk, no matter how safe and responsible you are. And the reason this message works so powerfully to the NRA rank and file is because, in truth, people who acquire guns legitimately and use them for lawful purposes tend to be safe, responsible and law-abiding. Because if they weren't, they wouldn't be able to buy a gun. It's as simple as that.

But the problem is that every time the cry goes up for more gun control, it's always in response to someone who acquired or used a gun illegally. Adam Lanza walked into the grammar school in Sandy Hook with, among other weapons, a SIG Sauer handgun. He was not yet twenty-one, which meant that even before he pulled the trigger he had broken the law. And virtually every gun-banger on the South Side of Chicago or in East LA also got their hands on guns illegally and used those guns to commit crimes; to wit, felonious assault ending in death. Here's the difference between highway deaths and gun deaths: highway deaths are fatalities, gun deaths (or at least the high-profile ones) are homicides. The number one cause of fatal highway accidents is carelessness. Last year less than 3% of all gun deaths were accidental. In every other case, the shooter meant to pull the trigger.

Not that most gun killings are crimes. To the contrary, of the 31,000 gun deaths in 2012, about one-third were homicides and two-thirds were suicides. Putting a gun to one's head or chest is an extremely effective way to end one's life; in fact people who try to end their lives with a gun are successful in 85% of the time, whereas people who take pills succeed in killing themselves only 5% of the time. Moreover, of all the suicides that occur in the United States each year, more than 50% involve guns, a higher percentage than all the other methods (jumping, drowning, etc.) combined. The preferred method everywhere else is hanging, but that's another reflection of the ease with which Americans can get their hands on guns.

But while illegal gun use does not account for a majority of gun deaths in the United States, it is the only thing that provokes calls for more gun control, either because the shooting produced multiple victims or a high-profile victim. And the moment that controlling guns *as a means of controlling gun violence* becomes a public issue, the average, law-abiding gun owner knows that his guns are in the cross-hairs of the anti-gun crowd. Because no matter how you slice it or dice it, everyone knows that if you drop the speed limit from 75 to 55 so that less people will drive at 90 mph, it's the people who always drive at the speed limit who will slow down the most. And if you pass a law that requires gun owners to register their guns, or register the private transfer of guns, or do anything to meet more requirements for gun ownership, it's the people who obey the law anyway that will have no choice but to obey the new law.

Why should someone living in Gassaway, West Virginia, or New Kensington, Pennsylvania, or Lexington, Nebraska, have to suffer the indignity of yet another legal requirement imposed on the ownership of his guns because the mother of a troubled teenager in Newtown, Connecticut let her son walk around with an AR-15? For that matter, why should the law-abiding gun owners of America have to follow more laws when everyone "knows" that there's no law in the inner cities at all? The NRA understands the emotions and viewpoints of their members and their well-worn slogan, "Guns Don't Kill People—People Kill People," has enough grains of truth in it both to establish the tone and set the content of every gun control debate.

There is, however, a different perspective on this issue, and it is this different perspective which shapes the approach of my book. It goes like this: after all the analysis, and all the data, and all the arguments pro and con, there is one simple issue that is consistently overlooked. The problem with guns is that every time someone pulls a trigger, a violent act has taken place. If you don't believe me, take a gun out of your drawer, or your pants pocket, or your gun safe, aim it at a window in your home, pull the trigger and see what happens. If the gun is loaded there will be a very loud noise followed by the crash of glass. That's not violent?

The most intriguing thing about guns is how very simple they really are. The materials and industrial processes have modernized, but the actual engineering and design of a handgun manufactured today is exactly the same as it was in the 1870's when smokeless powder cartridges allowed guns to be fired without reloading a separate powder charge after each shot. While the NRA may go to great lengths to pretend that firearms training is a serious business, there probably isn't a boy in the United States who hasn't played with a toy gun and hasn't seen hundreds, if not thousands of shootings on videos and TV. Picking up a real gun and pulling the trigger is a lot different than getting behind the wheel of a car, turning on the ignition and driving away. The latter activity really does take some training, the former can be accomplished without any practice or experience at all.

Last year I had an interesting experience with the internet coupon company known as GroupOn, or I should say multiple experiences in my gun shop that convinced me it was time to write this book. I was contacted by

Groupon and after some quick negotiations I agreed to advertise a "shooting experience" in the two-lane shooting range in the basement of my shop. The session consisted of a brief safety lesson followed by shooting first a 22-caliber and then a 9mm handgun at flat and what we call "spattering" targets. For a few extra bucks the shooter could also put some rounds through a plastic, life-size torso target that appears to actually drip blood from the wounds (it's some kind of red coloring). Groupon told me that this would be a way to increase sales in my shop and I assumed they were right. We also thought that the promotion, which was set to run for 3 days, would probably generate 100 coupon sales. Groupon and I were both wrong on both counts.

At the end of 3 days Groupon decided to extend the promotion because more than 200 coupons, most for multiple users, had been sold. When the promotion was completed, more than 800 people had signed up for a shooting experience at my shop. But the much bigger shock occurred when the Groupon buyers started coming in to redeem their coupons and actually shoot some guns. The typical customer in my retail store who comes in to buy a gun is a white male, 30-50 years old, probably just a high school education, a tradesman (carpenter, welder, etc.) and driving a small 4x4 truck. The typical Groupon customer was a female, age 20-30, college graduate, typical occupation being IT or medical technology. Why did they buy the Groupon? Because shooting a gun was always something they wanted to "try." How many of them actually owned guns? Virtually none. How many had previously shot a handgun? Virtually none. How many came back at some later point to buy a gun? Virtually none.

The truth is the GroupOn people were fascinated by the idea of shooting a gun. They had seen hundreds, if not thousands of shootings in movies and on TV. They had no interest in buying a gun, nor did they believe that they needed a gun for self-protection or for anything else. But almost without exception, they couldn't wait to fire a real gun and they couldn't get over how excited they were at being able to aim, pull the trigger, feel the gun jump in their hand and see a bullet hole downrange. Believe me, none of them would have come out to the shop if I had advertised a shooting session with a laser or video gun. It was the vicariousness of danger, of violence, that made them want to "try it out."

To deny that guns represent the highest and most efficient form of personal violence is to deny reality. That doesn't mean that people who own guns are necessarily more violent than people who don't. But the fact is that a gun is the perfect instrument for expressing anger because it immediately elevates the anger to the highest level of violence and, with rare exceptions due to lousy ammunition or user stupidity, it works every time. And while we acknowledge killing to be the most horrific form of human behavior, somehow when the act of killing involves a firearm, all the usual ways in which we talk or think about killing seem to disappear. For example, I don't recall any time over the last thirty years when the gun industry and its advocates have been more consumed with the issue of safe and responsible gun use. The National Shooting Sports Foundation, which lobbies for the gun manufacturers, has started a national campaign called ChildSafe which "promotes safe firearms handling and storage practices among all firearms owners." The campaign also features a pledge committing a firearms owner to using and storing guns safely, along with sending the owner's email address to the NSSF.

Nowhere in this campaign, nor in the NRA safety campaign known as Eddie Eagle, does the word "violence" appear, nor is there even an allusion to the threat of violence that exists when guns are accessible in public or private venues. In fact, the NRA compares gun safety to other types of consumer accident prevention, such as teaching children to behave safely around backyard pools, electrical outlets and household poison. The total number of deaths each year from all forms of electrocution, mostly job-related, is around one thousand. The total number of gun deaths that are ruled to be accidents is also around one thousand. But what about the other 30,000 gun deaths? The NRA and NSSF don't believe that this is their issue. After all, guns don't kill people, remember?

On the other hand, it's not clear that the gun control crowd has any better grasp on the reality of gun violence, given their recent propensity to venerate the 2nd Amendment in order to make "common cause" with all those law-abiding gun owners out there who just happen to own very lethal toys. This devotion to the constitutional protection of a hobby wouldn't be so bad were it not for the fact that the pro-gun folks brandish the sanctity of the 2nd Amendment whenever there's any talk about gun controls or any talk whatsoever by non-gun people about guns.

For example, the NRA tried to get a law enacted (and briefly succeeded in Florida) to charge physicians with a felony if they even inquired about the existence of firearms in the homes of their patients. The NRA's fatuous claim that the 2nd Amendment protected the "privacy" of gun owners to keep knowledge of their guns secret had no basis in law and, given the requirement that physicians talk to patients about all sorts of health risks, had no basis in common sense either. Yet the American Medical Association, in the company of 51 other medical societies and associations, sent an April 2013 letter to Harry Reid endorsing Dianne Feinstein's new assault weapons ban while, at the same time, noting their support for "protecting individual constitutional rights granted under the Second Amendment." Do such groups actually believe that if they join with the NRA in celebrating the virtues of the 2nd Amendment that the NRA will join with them in advocating more gun controls? Give me a break.

But if you want to really lose contact with reality when it comes to guns and how violent they are, try this one courtesy of the NRA. The voice for America's gun owners recently announced with great fanfare that they were releasing an "updated" version of their training course, *Refuse To Be a Victim*, that was originally developed by the "women of the NRA" in 1993. The program, according to the NRA, "directly addresses the goal of promoting both public safety, law and order, and reinforces the NRA's long-standing commitment to safety education." The Student Handbook runs 81 pages and covers such topics as home security, physical security in public places, automobile security and out-of-town travel security. It's chock full of interesting information on how to identify a potential threat, how to lock and guard your home, how to avoid carjackings and other dangers associated with automobiles, and it has a new section on internet security and measures to stop identity theft.

The home security section covers locks, alarms, outside and inside lighting, and measures to be taken when your home is unoccupied for a lengthy period of time but you would like it to appear as if someone is at home. In the section on home security, and in the entire handbook for that matter, the word "apartment" never appears, not even once. Nearly 50 million Americans live in apartments, but only states with large cities and a higher proportion of urban residents have more than 10% of their residents living in apartments, and this isn't exactly the demographic that responds to the NRA. The fact that 50% of all homicide victims are killed either in their apartments, or the hallways outside their apartments, or the street adjacent to the building in which their apartment is located is not the NRA's concern.

Nor does the NRA appear to be concerned about crime victims who happen to be women assaulted and often killed by intimate partners. Not only does the *Refuse to be a Victim* handbook give no advice on how to avoid or respond to domestic violence, you have to read all the way through the book to the very last page before the issue is mentioned at all. And what do they say about how to protect yourself from domestic violence? Nothing. The page simply contains a listing of some private and government organizations that give out information on domestic violence and stalking, even though the NRA "does not endorse all of the organizations' policies." What the single page does not mention is the fact that the NRA has opposed changes in state laws that would make it easier for law enforcement agencies to restrict or prohibit access to guns by people who are involved in a domestic dispute with a current for former intimate partner.

The NRA, the NSSF and the other pro-gun organizations aren't interested in curbing gun violence; they're interested in growing market share. The market consists primarily of rural or small-town whites, politically and socially conservative, who buy into the idea that gun violence is a big-city problem involving only minorities which, because every gun owner is or should be safe and responsible, doesn't make any difference to them at all. The fact that the number of white men living outside big cities who kill themselves each year is more than double the number of young black men who shoot someone else in the ghettos seems to escape everyone's notice. But why let facts mess up a good marketing campaign to sell more guns? Or for that matter, why let facts get in the way of a good advocacy campaign to get rid of those same guns? Don't worry folks, no matter which side of the gun debate you're on, I'm going to talk about both.

CHAPTER 2

WHY DOES THE NRA WIN?

"You go into these small towns in Pennsylvania and, like a lot of small towns in the Midwest, the jobs have been gone now for 25 years and nothing's replaced them. And it's not surprising then they get bitter, they cling to guns or religion or antipathy to people who aren't like them or anti-immigrant sentiment or anti-trade sentiment as a way to explain their frustrations."

—Barack Obama

Not necessarily an untrue picture of life in many small towns in rural Pennsylvania and elsewhere. Which is where most guns in America can be found. And which is where most NRA members live. But Obama the candidate got it completely wrong if he really believed that the people in these towns were clinging to their guns because they had nothing else—no jobs, no futures, no hope. The NRA's membership hasn't been thrown into the rural underclass by the collapse of small-town economies. People who come into a gun shop five or six times a year and walk out each time with a five or six-hundred dollar gun don't have trouble making the rent. They don't pay rent. They own.

No wonder the President and his allies got clobbered when they tried to push through a gun control bill in the aftermath of Sandy Hook. They really didn't know who they were dealing with.

The average NRA member is a white male who owns his home in a small or medium-sized town, is married and works as a tradesman, a semi-skilled craftsman or industrial manager. He doesn't usually own a business but he thinks and behaves like a small business owner: prudent, cautious, Republican and risk averse. If he's under 50 he probably finished high school and his wife may have gone to college. His idea of a family outing is to get everyone into the 4x4, roll over to Home Depot and then stop for lunch at Mickey Dee's. He owns his own home and, let's not forget, the home contains multiple guns. If you ask him he'll tell you that the guns are all locked up and safely stored, because whether they are or not, he knows that it's the right thing to say. Finally, he owns guns because he always owned guns and because his father owned guns and left them to him. He may have hunted with his father but the chances are less likely that he hunts or that his kids will go out hunting with or without him.

Most important about the average NRA member, more important than even his ownership of multiple guns, is that he identifies himself as a gun person; that is, someone whose interests and activities revolve around guns. We used to call people like this "hobbyists," denoting an active interest in the acquisition and use of certain kinds of consumer products with which he or she could relax, enjoy himself or herself or the company of like-minded other hobbyists. If you go to a gun show today you'll see the same types who flocked to computer shows twenty years ago, or ham radio shows forty or fifty years ago. And like computers or ham radios, everyone had their favorite piece of equipment and could trick it out, or fix it when it broke, or trade it for another item that they had "always" wanted and needed.

Gun hobbyists are also, for the most part, gun collectors. They don't collect guns the way wealthy folks collect wine or art; they collect guns in the sense that they own *lots* of them. There are certain guns that have become "collectibles;" i.e., they are so unique that they have a certain inflated value. But their value is usually tied to their history based on who owned the gun—a shotgun owned by Clyde Barrow, a rifle owned by Teddy Roosevelt, a special Colt given to some Russian Czar or a Walther pistol carried by Joseph Goebbels, and so forth. When I first started buying guns in the 1970's you could send ten dollars to Colt with the serial number of your Colt gun and they would send you a letter embossed with a lithograph of the Colt factory containing the particulars of when your gun was manufactured and the identity of the original owner. I was very impressed to discover that my Colt Single Action Army revolver was shipped to a hardware store in Kansas in 1883, or maybe it was 1886.

My personal gun collection numbered, at its high-water mark, around 50 guns. I sold almost all of them to get the money to buy a Harley Low Rider. I sold the Low Rider when I realized that the only women I managed to pick up with my bike were my teenage daughters. Owning 50 guns put me at the low end of gun hobbyists that I knew. One family whose two boys worked in my retail store have at least 300 guns lying around their house. There's a famous country-western singer who, between him and his brother, probably owns 500 guns. The guy who used to own my gun shop loved World War I Mauser carbines and kept more than 1,000 of them neatly stacked in his basement. That may sound like a lot of money tied up in old military surplus weapons, but he probably paid about thirty bucks for each one. Maybe he was planning to invade Poland.

This is an entirely subjective analysis and is based on nothing more than personal observations over many years and discussions at many gun shows, but I would suspect that if the NRA really does have 4 million members, then between them they probably own between 50 and 100 million guns. Think I'm wrong? Don't bet on it. I have four customers who I know are members of the NRA. Over the last twelve years I have sold these guys—together—at least 100 guns. How many more have they purchased privately or from other dealers? I have one customer who is a machinist. He makes a nice buck. He's married to a woman who also earns a good living and none of their kids are living (or sponging off of them) at home. He works four, ten-hour days and on Fridays gets in his 4x4 or, in good weather, on his Harley and drives around to his four favorite gun dealers; two in Massachusetts and two in New Hampshire. He buys at least one gun on every Friday excursion; I have sold him at least ten guns in the last six months. He's not a member of the NRA but he's worried about more laws that will restrict his access to firearms. Why shouldn't he be worried?

Which brings us to the single most vexing question about guns: how many of the damn things are really out there? The "accepted" number is usually put at between 250 and 300 million, a figure derived by starting with a National Institute of Justice estimate of 192 million as of 1995 increased by the total number of guns manufactured and imported each year as reported to the ATF. Before I get into the specifics of this data, note that both sides of the gun debate have an interest in inflating the number as much as possible; the anti-gun people to justify the need for more controls, the pro-gun folks to prove that guns are a mainstream product that everyone owns or should own.

But let's go back to the Institute of Justice number. Everybody appears to accept this number and everyone overlooks two basic problems. The first is the idea of deriving information about gun ownership through a randomized telephone survey. According to the NIJ, the methodology for picking respondents was based on employing "a list-assisted random-digit-dial sampling method, in which every residential telephone number had the same likelihood of being selected." But as we have seen, gun transfer registrations, as shown by NICS checks, are not randomly distributed throughout the United States. They are concentrated in certain states and, since the NICS system wasn't fully operational until 1999, this distribution could not have been known when the Institute of Justice conducted its survey in 1994-95.

The second problem is that asking about guns in a randomized survey isn't the same thing as asking about the ownership of automobiles or the existence of pets. Most gun owners assume that anyone other than another gun owner who asks about guns is doing so for some nefarious purpose; i.e., collecting information on gun owner identification as a prelude to some sort of confiscation program, or allowing gun owners to be targets of further gun control laws. These views are so ingrained in the gun business that I can't imagine how any telephone survey, randomized or not, would necessarily yield valid data.

But with all those caveats, let's assume that the survey was fairly realistic and that the subsequent manufacturing and importing information is also reliable. There's still a bigger question that needs to be answered and until this moment has never been asked; namely, should we be talking about how many guns comprise the American consumer arsenal, or should we be talking about *functional* guns? It really makes a difference if there are two, three or twenty guns sitting in the basement of grandpa's house if it turns out that half of them don't work either because they're rusted, or broken, or if they were all thrown out when the old man was carted off to the nursing home and the real estate salvaged the entire contents of the basement to make room for a new furnace in order to re-sell the home.

Think I'm exaggerating? I'm not. One of the major demographic shifts occurring in America is the movement of younger people out of smaller towns into suburbs or cities, leaving behind the old, the poor and the uneducated —the gun and religion-clingers, if you will. My gun shop is located in a town of 10,000 people, many of whom once worked in the red-brick sneaker factory and paper mill that are both slowly settling into dust. The only young people living in the town are the ones who didn't finish school and are too unskilled to leave; the rest all went away to college and then got jobs in Boston which is 60 miles away and teeming with young people like themselves. They come back from time to time to say hello, and when the older generation disappears, they return to settle personal and property affairs. The house is put up for sale, the car is towed away, a quick glance yields a picture or personal keepsake that needs to be taken back home, and everything else ends up at the dump. Including the guns.

In the twelve years that I have owned a retail gun shop I have probably purchased more than 1,000 used guns and taken at least another 3,000 as partial payment on a gun that went out the door. I would estimate that at least one-quarter of these 4,000 guns needed to be repaired or have parts replaced in order to function again. The funny thing is that I don't remember the last time that anyone ever tried to sell or trade a gun that had been shot more than "a few" times. Guns don't have odometers like cars but I can usually tell whether a gun has been fired a lot or a little based on powder fouling around the barrel and a few other tricks of the trade that I don't want to explain. Okay, so it's only been shot two or three (hundred) times.

Not only do older guns tend to rust or break, but finding parts for a Remington rifle made in the 1950's is a little like trying to replace a carburetor in a Plymouth Fury. Remember carburetors? How about the Plymouth Fury? If you're lucky and the local junk yard hasn't yet compacted the last Fury they took in, you might be able to creak open the hood and find a usable carburetor. Ditto with older guns. Once a gun goes out of production the manufacturer waits a few years and then stops making parts. Ammunition for older guns also begins to disappear once a particular model moves from the store shelves to the basement closet. For years and years Savage Arms made a great, medium-range deer rifle in lever action known as the "Savage 99" because it was first produced in 1899, although a predecessor model came out in 1895. In various configurations and various calibers the gun was produced until 1998 and was chambered in just about every medium-range hunting caliber, most notably something called the .303 Savage. There must be at least several million 99's floating around but walk into a gun shop today and see how many boxes of .303 Savage the store has for sale. If you can't find ammunition, do you really possess a functional gun?

Of the nearly 200 million guns that the Institute of Justice presumed to be in private hands in 1995, it is impossible to derive an accurate number for how many could actually be shot. I'm going to discuss the economics of the gun business in a later chapter but take it as a given that one of the reasons the gun business has always operated on thin margins is because the damn things just don't wear out. They may be covered with rust and may not actually fire when you pull the trigger, but they don't just shrivel up and disappear. Since the Institute of Justice did not ask any questions designed to identify the type or age of firearms that were allegedly sitting in 40% of the homes they surveyed, I'm going to go along with my own experience and assume that as many as 50 million of those guns weren't functional at all.

I'm willing to bet that if we take all the guns owned by NRA members (120 million), add to that total the number of non-functional guns owned by non-NRA members (20 million), and add to that total the guns that are sitting in gun stores as yet unsold (500,000 to 1 million), we probably end up with somewhere around 100 million other guns. Which means that the per capita ownership of guns in the United States isn't 88 guns per 100 residents, which is the current number advanced by everyone who has a stake in promoting either more or less gun control, but somewhere around 30 per hundred residents or even less, which puts the U.S. in line with Canada, Austria and Germany, in other words, countries that are always touted as having much less gun violence because they have many fewer guns.

The point is that just as the geography of gun ownership in the United States is skewed towards certain parts of the country, so the number of guns owned by Americans is also skewed towards people who like to play with guns—the hobbyists—and most of the serious hobbyists are members of the NRA. Hobbyists, no matter what type of hobby, tend to take care of their toys. They are more careful with how they are used, how they are stored, and how they are protected from abuse or theft. They also tend to buy and sell their toys from and to other hobbyists—that's what being a hobbyist is all about. Nobody ever takes up ham radio because they hope to get a message from the Titanic, although every once in a great while a ham radio operator actually picks up a broadcast sent by someone in distress. They take up ham radio or some other hobby because it's their way of being social, of identifying themselves and belonging to a group, or it's just something they learned how to do.

These are the reasons that people own guns. But that's not why they "cling" to the guns. The President could certainly understand the hobbyist mentality; it's my impression that golf has become a hobby for him. But "clinging" is a little different, and his remark in that respect illustrated a very different issue and one that he and most of the gun control crowd simply cannot and will not understand. Even though recent polls indicate that a majority of gun owners are purchasing guns for personal defense, the same polls taken a generation ago indicated that hunting was still the primary reason for gun ownership in the United States. And this would have been true whether a poll was dated from thirty years ago, or sixty years ago, or at any time since guns first started to be sold. The fact that the younger generation would rather sit at home and play video games than go out into the woods or fields with Dad and Grandpa doesn't mean that the activity of hunting as a definer of family history and culture has disappeared. And it is within hunting—its rituals, practices and rewards—that the difference between people who own guns and people who don't own guns is most pronounced.

Going into the woods and bagging a white-tail is not a casual, everyday sort of thing. And that's what hunting's all about in the gun-clinging communities of America. It takes knowledge, advance planning, cooperation and dedication. You have to find a good spot, set up a blind or a stand, scent the area, make sure you're downwind and, most of all, make sure you can get a clean shot. Because the one thing you really don't want to do is go chasing a wounded white-tail into the woods, because there's a good chance you'll be scrambling through the thickets and brush for days on end. And when you finally find the animal and finish it off, you'd better have someone with you because unless you're ready to drag 150 pounds of venison back to your truck, you've just spent the day giving the woodland predators the fixings for a good meal.

This isn't the only kind of hunting that goes on in and out of the United States. If you have a few bucks and want to turn a hunt into a family vacation you can always go out to the Grand Tetons, book a suite in the Jackson Lake or Jenny Lake Lodge and a guide and outfitter will pick you up, transport you out to where the elk roam inside a fenced multi-acre hunting "farm" and, for a couple of thousand you'll be guaranteed a good shot. And just in case you haven't been practicing your shooting skills much lately because it's tough to sight a rifle out of the 36th floor of a Manhattan hi-rise, there's no need to worry because as you squeeze the trigger your friendly outfitter is sitting next to you and he's squeezing his trigger too. Trophy hunting is kind of like sky diving; every real man wants to say he did it at least once.

But when most gun clingers talk about hunting they mean deer hunting and they mean going into their local woods. In most white-tail states the season usually lasts 2-3 months; some states like South Carolina let you hunt between September and January, some northeast states like Massachusetts limit white-tail gun hunts to two weeks or less. But generally speaking, the gun-rich states with large, lowland coastal deer populations have open seasons that last several months and if you decide to hunt with archery equipment or flintlocks the season extends even longer.

Even if the younger kids don't go into the woods for deer any longer, they remember when their father went with his father and maybe they even give in to the old man and go out once or twice again. But remember who's going into the woods to get those white-tails. It's not Mr. Joe College or Ms. Med-Tech Specialist. It's not the kids who moved away. It's the kids and their parents who are still sitting in those gun-clinging towns. And for many of these folks, hunting is one of the few things they can enjoy that doesn't cost an arm and a leg and, more important, is a true test of their personal skills. Because it doesn't take a lot of skill to drive a truck, or dig a ditch, or pave a driveway, or do one of the hundred other service tasks that have taken the place of the red-brick factory jobs that used to exist in these towns; jobs whose disappearance, according to the President, heightens the desire to cling to the guns.

But what the President and the non-gun owning population of America doesn't understand is that even when they still worked those small-town factory jobs it was the white-tail hunt, not the paycheck, that defined and brightened their lives. Planning and executing a hunt was a job well done, a project completed on time, a skill-set that could be taught by father to son. Know what you usually got for showing up at the factory early and busting your hump to get the product out early onto the dock? What you usually got for your efforts was a lay-off notice because if your work was finished ahead of schedule there was no reason to keep the machine running and pay you until the next order arrived.

If you think I'm overstating the case you've probably lived in a big city or a nice suburb all your life. You no doubt went to college, maybe even professional school, and the only work you do with your hands is to punch keys on the laptop or the iPad. Hunting, not just as a sport or for recreation is a key signpost in situating the cultural borders between gun owners and non-gun owners. And more to the point, it's an activity that can't be carried out without a gun. Oh yes, you can try and bag a deer with a bow and arrow if you're willing to sit on your rear end for hours at a time and hope that the animal comes close enough so that you can almost reach out and stick the arrow into his hide. Or you can load up a black-powder rifle and make sure that the shot hits home because if you miss, the deer will be in the next county before you get the gun loaded and primed again.

But there's nothing quite like walking into the woods with a Winchester 30-30 rifle or a Remington 870 pump, slinging the gun over your shoulder, tucking a small, plastic chair under your arm and carrying a sandwich, a can of beer and maybe even a book to your spot, then sitting down and waiting, listening for the tell-tale "swish" which tells you that the guy you're waiting for may be even closer than you think. I once was sitting out in the woods in Fairfield County, South Carolina, hunting some land that belonged to the town magistrate, Harold Hill. I didn't have to pay for the privilege because before I went to my spot I had agreed to give the magistrate's son, Freddie, half the meat from the kill. And the good news is that if I got a big one, Freddie would come into the woods to help us pull it out. So I sat there all day and came back the next day and sat again. My friend Sherrill Smith was sitting in another spot halfway up the same hill. And another hunting buddy, Arley (but we called him "Pat") Patterson was alongside the creek-bed down yonder.

Sherrill had scouted this land earlier in the year and he noticed that there were abundant tracks leading down to the water so he marked the dirt road going into the forest, learned that the entire mountain was owned by Judge Hill, and sent me off to see the Judge and make the deal. Once we got access to the land, we went out there and I sat for a day and a half quietly waiting, sitting, dozing off and occasionally reading a book (I think it was *Sideshow: Kissinger, Nixon and the Destruction of Cambodia* by William Shawcross) until I suddenly heard a very slight "swish." And very slowly turning around, I saw a red fox standing just behind my chair, looking intently into my face. But the moment our eyes met there was a louder noise, almost a "whoosh" kind of noise behind him and the biggest, the damn biggest buck I had ever seen came striding out of a thicket to my left.

The problem was that my rifle, a Remington 700 in 270 Winchester, was leaning against a tree and I knew that to reach it I would have had to stand up. Maybe the deer knew this and maybe he didn't. But what for sure he couldn't know, this extraordinary 12-point monster, was that my lap held both the book I was reading and a 4-inch Colt Python revolver chambered for 357 magnum. And it wasn't just any 357, by the way. It was a 357 round that had been handloaded by my friend Sherrill Smith, who was considered one of the greatest handloaders in the entire state of South Carolina. And he handloaded this ammunition specifically for deer season because if you take a 158-grain, semi-wadcutter lead bullet and plop it on top of a shell case holding 2400 rifle powder packed right to the brim, you have a cartridge which will knock over any white-tail deer within 100 yards.

My Remington 700 which took a lot of whitetails.

So I raised the Python and got off two shots before the animal slipped behind some brush and was out of sight. He had been headed down the hill to the water and almost made it, even with the two slugs inside him, but Pat Patterson was waiting at the river bottom and finished him off. He hit the animal on the side of his jaw and almost took its head off at a distance of about 40 yards. But this magnificent animal kept moving, cleared the stream and we finally found him about a quarter-mile beyond where Pat had tried to gun him down. When we caught up to him he still was alive. Sherrill ended it with a quick knife thrust but talk about a will to live. And we did talk about that animal again and again for as long as we remained friends.

Now that I've finished the story about how we bagged that deer I want to ask and then answer a question. Earlier I said that my friend Sherrill was one of the greatest ammo handloaders in South Carolina. He was also considered to be one of the best white-tail hunters in the state. How did I know this? Because someone told me.

And in hunting and in guns it's all about what someone else tells you. Shooters and hunters sometimes read, but mostly they talk. It's a very verbal culture because you're always comparing your experience to the experience of someone else because what you learn from someone else can make you a better shooter or a better hunter. And that's the whole point: to accomplish something, to do it well. And when you do it well enough, other hunters and shooters respect you, and acknowledge that you have skills which they wish they had. That's what we get out of hunting and shooting. That's why we cling to those guns. And that's something that people who don't own guns will never understand. But it's something the NRA understands very well.

Last summer I went to two gun shows, one in Lancaster, PA and the other in Cobleskill, NY. The Lancaster show was held in the town's Convention Center which looked about big enough to hold a convention of the county Girl Scouts or maybe the 4-H clubs. The Cobleskill show was held at the county fair site in a large, open area with a roof but no walls that was used for displaying live animals during the fairs. Both shows featured more non-gun vendors than gun dealers, this was particularly the case in Cobleskill where I was told that the county sheriff "doesn't like handguns." The gun tables at Cobleskill were manned for the most part by seniors and their wives who evidently all knew each other, judging by how much time they spent walking around and gabbing with the other exhibitors. Many of the men and some of the women wore baseball hats emblazoned either with the logo of some long-ago military unit or the logo of the NRA. The Lancaster show was larger, and had more licensed dealers, some of whom made their livings or part of their livings by displaying and selling at weekend gun shows throughout the year. Prominent at both shows were food and snack areas and I cannot say that concerns about obesity were much in evidence among the vendors or the visitors at either show.

What was of concern to just about everyone at these shows was whether they could find a particular part: a screw, a bolt, a spring, a trigger or a barrel for their favorite gun. I'm describing these two gun shows because they are the last two shows that I attended so my memory is very sharp. But over the years I have probably shopped, wandered through and been a vendor with a table at more than fifty gun shows in at least ten different states. And with the exception of a couple of the mega events in Western states like the shows in Tulsa, Phoenix and Houston, gun shows are all the same: tag sales featuring guns and gun-related stuff, most of it used and plenty of it not so much put out for sale but as a way for the owners to sit around, gab with their friends and have a good time.

There were probably 30 gun shows throughout the United States the weekend of June 29-30, 2013. They were held in places like Fredericksburg, Virginia; Bremerton, Washington; Pasadena, Texas; Live Oak, Texas; York, Pennsylvania; Lawrenceville, Georgia; Sidney, Ohio and Ozark, Arkansas—media and cultural centers of the world. These shows had 300-400 tables, usually 4x6 or 4x8, which probably means 100 people selling guns since most dealers take multiple tables. How many people attend these shows? On a good weekend a show that has 300-400 tables can usually pull in 5 or 6 thousand people of whom probably half are too young to buy a gun. That still adds up to a lot of people—do the arithmetic as Bill Clinton would say and we have maybe upwards of 8 million men, women and children trundling through arenas, convention centers, motel meeting rooms and outdoor spaces attending gun shows each year.

Gun shows are family affairs. As noted earlier, the most popular display at the show is usually the stand selling hot dogs, drinks, cotton candy and other treats and snacks that can easily be gulped down while walking down this aisle or that. Military memorabilia used to be a big seller at the shows, in particular Nazi medals, helmets and uniforms and other stuff from World War II, but just as the number of WWII veterans is about to drop under 1,000, so the interest in a war that most high school kids don't even study is also on the wane. Many of the gun shows also feature craft items related to guns, in particular knives and jewelry, along with the ubiquitous t-shirt vendors who can concoct a mountainous display of cotton wherever people are walking around with a few bucks to spare.

You would think with all the hue and cry about conducting background checks at gun shows that the various promoters, most of whom run multiple shows, would have long ago formed a trade association and hired a K Street firm to push their case on Capitol Hill. The fact that they have not done so is perhaps one of the reasons why gun shows, in form and function, are so misunderstood. I don't recall the last congressional session, for example, where Senator Feinstein and some of her colleagues *didn't* re-introduce their bill to "plug" the gun show "loophole." And what loophole are they talking about? The one that allegedly allows anyone to walk into a gun show without the slightest bit of legal compliance or regulation and purchase a gun. Let's examine this loophole a little more closely.

In my experience, most of the people who rent a table or tables and sell guns at a show are either holders of the standard, commercial Federal Firearms License (FFL), or they hold the Federal Collector's License known as the C&R. The C&R License, which stands for Collectibles and Relics, is issued by the ATF at a cost of $30 and is valid for three years. It is issued following the same background check that is required for any NICS transaction, does not require the licensee to operate out of a commercial location, and allows for interstate shipment of guns between federal licensees. To be classified as a collectible, a gun must be fifty years old at the time of transaction, and that's it. The gun doesn't have to be worth anything, or listed in any kind of register like the register that is used to list old homes. It just needs to be fifty years old, which means that every day more guns can be transferred with a C&R. There are approximately 60,000 C&R licenses in the United States, and while the ATF in theory can inspect a C&R licensee who by law must keep a record of all transactions, I have never heard of any C&R ever being greeted at his front door by the ATF.

Here's the catch: guns acquired under a C&R license can only be sold to other C&R license-holders or to other federal firearms licensees. But many of the transactions that take place at gun shows involve the acquisition and disposition of C&R guns from one C&R-holder to another. Most of these "collectors" have collections that are worth next to nothing. In fact, they often buy old, broken guns for the pleasure of restoring them to near-working condition. They're hobbyists, remember? Sitting out in the garage or down in the basement and rubbing a chamois cloth over a slightly rusted receiver of an old Winchester shotgun can fill up a whole day, plus the wife knows where you are if she needs a quick bottle of cooking oil from the store. Believe me when I tell you that I could count on the fingers of one and one-half hands the number of times I have seen real collectible firearms at gun shows.

I'm not saying that illegal sales don't take place at shows. I'm not saying that there aren't rogue dealers here and there. Some states impose licensing and record-keeping requirements on federal dealers beyond what is required by the ATF, and the history of government regulation of anything is that whatever or whomever is regulated always results in a certain amount of activity going, shall we say, underground. When the Bourbon Kings imposed a tax on salt imports in the 17th Century, smuggling became the largest occupational category in the coastal province of Languedoc. Gee, what a surprise.

But the whole point about gun shows is, as I mentioned earlier, they are family affairs which make them social affairs. Most gun show promoters rent the same building one weekend every three or four months. They've run the same show for years. The local police chief gives them the same permit and a couple of officers turn an extra detail by standing or sitting at the front door. The local town paper runs the ad with the "dollar off admission" coupon that is honored whether you remember to bring it or not. The local parking lot fills up for five bucks a vehicle on a weekend which otherwise would probably be dead. And of course let's not forget the family that runs the concession stand and pockets some of the cash. The most important point about a gun show however, is that people don't come to buy guns. That doesn't mean they don't buy guns. It means that it really doesn't matter whether or not they buy a gun.

The reason it doesn't matter is very simple: most of the folks who come to the shows already own lots of guns. And they come to the shows because they feel comfortable talking to other people who own lots of guns. I sold guns at several shows and every time someone stood in front of my table and picked up a gun, someone came up next to him and either started talking about the fact that he owned the same kind of gun or that he had sold the same kind of gun, or he had decided not to buy the same kind of gun, or something else involving that gun. Many times the people know each other, many times they do not. Doesn't matter. The tie that binds is the gun. And the fact that two people can talk to each other about the same gun makes them equals, makes them respect one another, makes them share a camaraderie that is embedded in the gun that one of them is holding.

I said above that gun shows are family affairs. They are also something else. They are remarkably fertile breeding grounds for the NRA. Walk into any gun show and the first thing you'll see is a banner promoting the NRA. Will they have a table where they sell memberships to the few people at the show who aren't already members? Probably. Will they give away a free membership in a raffle whose tickets are sold to benefit some worthy, pro-gun cause? Probably. Will you find some NRA literature on every table in the hall? You betcha. After all, no NRA, no gun show. And no gun show, no hobby and no guns. The NRA knows how gun owners think about guns because the NRA never misses an opportunity to talk to them about their guns.

The NRA also tells them how to think about nuisances like background checks. Many of the transactions that take place at gun shows don't involve cash. Listen to the conversations between people at a show and you'll suddenly realize that you're actually standing in the middle of a big swap meet. Gun owners usually divide their collections into three groups of guns: the guns they'll never give up, the guns that they'll get rid of because either they have more than one of that kind or they don't want to shoot it any more, and the guns that are just real junk. The junkers can be traded or replaced at any time and not necessarily for other guns. Are those hub caps he's walking around with equal in value to my old Mauser 98? Should I dump the Ted Williams Sears Roebuck single-shot for a

Chinese bayonet? At least those markings look like Chinese characters although I'm not really sure. As for the guns that I just don't want anymore because something at the show has caught my eye, I can do a quick deal selling my Remington 590 for two hundred bucks to the guy standing in front of the table over there and that will give me enough dough to pick up that 410 Ithaca over here. And if I decide I don't like shooting the 410 I'll bring it back to the next show and exchange it for some other gun.

Do you really think that extending background checks to those kinds of transactions will do anything to keep guns off the streets? If you're not a gun owner you simply can't imagine why *any* honest citizen would be afraid to let a dealer call the FBI to conduct a background check on the transfer of a gun. But that's because you're not a gun owner. You don't go to gun shows and you don't understand that once you get inside a show, it's "us" versus "them." And the "them" consists of everyone who wants to make a federal case out of what's nothing more than a hobby and a fun-filled afternoon. If questioned by a telephone poll, most people who identify themselves as owning guns will always tell the pollster that they "support" background checks. But that's no different from saying that drinking and driving don't mix. The same gun owners who agree that background checks are a "good thing" will also tell you that the NRA is fighting for their "right" to own a gun. Is there a contradiction between those two points of view? Believe me, the gun owners couldn't care less.

Guns shows aren't the only social venues that exist because of guns. And the problem with gun shows is you can look at the guns, touch the guns, hold the guns, play with the guns, but you can't *shoot* the guns. If you want to shoot a gun, you usually have two choices. If you own a big enough back yard and the town doesn't have an ordinance prohibiting same, you can go outside and bang away. I live 75 miles outside of Boston and I sit on 15 acres, so I can shoot to my heart's content. But most people don't have access to so much open space around their homes, so they shoot at a local range or join the town's sportsman's club. And like many religious denominations where the same town has two or three congregations because "we" didn't like "them" or whatever, some small towns even have more than one club. Wisconsin has more than 200 shooting clubs and ranges, ditto Florida and Kentucky, while Texas has more than 500 clubs and that's a state with lots of empty space.

But what attracts shooters to join these clubs is the same thing that brings them out to the gun shows time after time. There's a friendship and a bond that develops between people who like to do the same thing. And the bond gets particularly strong when they are doing something they really enjoy. Will you find an NRA poster on the walls of what are probably more than 5,000 shooting clubs and ranges in the United States? You might not find an NRA presence in every single clubhouse. But if you don't, it's probably because they repainted the walls last year and forgot to stick the poster back up. And as I'll talk about in the next chapter, the shooting clubhouse is really sacred space for the NRA, because this is where almost all the NRA-sponsored training of new shooters invariably takes place.

The NRA's development of this grass-roots support network uniting gun shows and sportsman's clubs is not a new phenomenon. After all, the organization began as a way to promote civilian firearms training and marksmanship in the decades after the Civil War. The first NRA president was a Union general named George Wingate, who established the organization in New York City, which was his home town. The NRA remained largely a local affair until the beginning of the 20th Century, when an aggressive campaign was developed to partner with the American Legion, Boy Scouts of America, 4-H Clubs and other civic/patriotic groups to spread the gospel of shooting throughout the United States. In 1955, my brother and I joined the NRA rifle club that practiced in the basement shooting range of my brother's junior high school. Most Fridays, after a practice or a match, he and I would take one of the .22 range rifles home for the weekend to clean it and dry-fire it to our heart's content. This meant walking about one mile from his school to our home, toting what was clearly a rifle in a little, cloth sack.

Were we living in Topeka, Kansas or Abilene, Texas or Greenville, South Carolina? *We lived on Hamilton Street in the middle of Washington, D.C.* And the rifle we dragged home was no doubt a 1903 Springfield that was originally built for the U.S. Army but was used as a training rifle so it had been re-chambered from the military's 30-06 caliber to a more manageable 22. There were thousands of these rifles rusting away in government arsenals after World War I, and they were given (note: given) by the U.S. Government to the NRA who then sold them to shooting clubs for five bucks apiece. Think the NRA and the Federal Government have always been at odds with one another over guns? Think again.

The first time that the NRA proclaimed the Federal Government to be its 2nd Amendment *bête noir* was in 1994, when the Brady bill and the assault weapons ban were debated and passed. The NRA had actually won an important but quiet victory in 1976 when they persuaded Congress to exempt firearms and ammunition from the scope of the Consumer Product Safety Act because the law, as originally written, would not have allowed the Consumer Product Safety Commission to regulate ammunition anyway. What this meant was that firearms manufacturers did not have to worry about Federal oversight of gun design from a safety perspective, even though by definition guns could be considered as inherently unsafe. It also meant that discussions about gun safety would focus on the behavior of people who used guns, not the manner in which guns functioned themselves, regardless of who used them.

But in 1993 the NRA, which had initially supported the 1968 Gun Control Act that contained the inert background check procedure, now reversed its stance in an effort to prevent the live background check procedures promoted by the Brady group and other gun-control organizations. It was the failure of the pro-gun forces to prevent the enactment of the Brady bill, along with the passage of the assault weapons ban the following year, which produced a new and more vigorous effort by the NRA to build grass-roots support against gun control both at the state and federal level. Much of this activity followed the elevation in 1991 of Wayne LaPierre to head the organization, a move brought about by dissatisfaction with the lack of aggressiveness of the previous administration. Ironically, the father of the current NRA president, George Porter, Jr., was considered part of the less-than-tough-enough group that was ousted by LaPierre and his allies in 1991.

The strategy developed by the NRA to build the organization after the battles of the 90's, both of which they lost, consisted of two parts: on the one hand, making gun owners feel that they were a special group of people because they understood the historical, cultural and social value of guns; on the other hand, attacking every gun control proposal as an assault on the 2nd Amendment, while also trying to eliminate or loosen legal gun restrictions that were already on the books. As regards the membership, the NRA promoted the theme, "Guns Don't Kill People—People Kill People," and pushed for the strict application of mandatory sentences for violent crime, additional penalties for crimes involving the use of guns and harsher sentences for repeat offenders. They also inaugurated the "Don't Lie for the Other Guy" campaign, and urged storefront gun retailers to post public warnings about straw sale purchases in the public areas of their shops. These PR efforts and others drew a clear line between pro-gun and anti-gun advocates that would define the position of both camps from then down to the present day: the NRA and its allies viewed and continues to view the gun problem as an issue of controlling the access to guns by certain types of people; the opposition groups viewed and continues to view the problems in terms of controlling access to the guns themselves.

Along with efforts to fight gun control laws at the federal and state level, the NRA also began to widen the legality of concealed weapons permits which, until the 1990's, were granted without special conditions or requirements in only a handful of states. In fact, more states had laws prohibiting than allowing the carrying of handguns, even though the Western states were more flexible when it came to transporting rifles visibly in motor vehicles, particularly small trucks. Over the next twenty years, the NRA successfully lobbied various state legislatures to the point that by 2013, all 50 states had laws on the books that allowed some form of concealed carry of guns.

In addition to making concealed carry permits more available to the public, the NRA also fought to prohibit or limit the ability of gun license issuing agencies to exercise discretion as regards the granting of a license to own or carry a gun. Generally speaking, legislatures and courts in many states traditionally held to the view that the decision as to who should be able to own or carry a firearm in any community was best left to the local police who, after all, were not only responsible for public safety, but also usually kept their eyes on local residents who were considered threats to the community, even though they may not have yet actually committed a crime. Over time the vesting of ultimate authority to allow gun ownership came to be divided between states where gun licensing was based on a "shall issue" rule, as opposed to states where gun licensing proceeded on a "may issue" rule, the difference being that "shall issue" jurisdictions were required to grant gun licenses if the applicant met the stated, legal requirements for gun ownership, as opposed to "may issue" jurisdictions that allowed the issuing authority discretion in terms of license issuance even if the applicant's legal record and personal history did not disqualify him from being granted a license.

The NRA has vigorously promoted the idea that "may issue" practices are an infringement of the 2nd Amendment, even though, as I will explain below, the definitive 2008 2nd Amendment ruling did not apply constitutional protection to taking guns out of the home. Nevertheless, the NRA and its allies have consistently tried to use the 2nd Amendment as the lever for widening legal gun use and promoting the notion that guns are as normal and mainstream as any other type of consumer product. To be fair, in many states whose concealed carry laws are based on "shall issue" approval procedures, law enforcement in many local jurisdictions still claim the right to withhold or add specific conditions to concealed licenses, forcing an applicant in many cases to endure both the extra waiting time and legal costs of pushing a concealed carry application over the head of the local authorizing agency.

Where the NRA really began to show its muscle and clout, however, was not so much in the protecting of gun owners but in the attack on gun manufacturers. The first assault took place in 1989 when Bill Ruger, without doubt the single most iconic name in the gun world since John Browning, sent a letter to congressmen voicing his support for the limitation of gun magazine capacity that ultimately became part of the assault weapons ban signed into law by President Clinton in September, 1994.

Bill Ruger – Brooklyn boy who made lots of nice guns.

In fact, Ruger had designed a very popular semi-automatic rifle, the Mini-14, which although different in both look and function from military-style rifles, was nevertheless considered by many shooters to be part of the assault-type family because it was chambered in the military .223 caliber. But Bill Ruger never allowed his company to ship the gun with more than a 5-shot magazine, even though after-market companies produced hi-cap Mini-14 magazines that held 50 rounds or more. In any case, Ruger's letter endorsing the idea of restricting hi-cap magazines provoked a fury in the gun world, and while the NRA refrained from directly attacking him, they nevertheless engineered a back-door deal in which Ruger publicly apologized for the letter, stating that it was his own personal opinion and did not reflect company policy.

Ten years later the NRA squared off against another gun manufacturer who appeared to be parting ways with the rest of the industry and gun consumers over the issue of gun control, and in this instance they spared no effort in attacking and eventually forcing their targeted opponent back into line. The target in this case was Smith & Wesson, until that time the premier handgun company not only in the United States but throughout the world. What happened was that after the assault weapons ban was passed in 1994, the Clinton Administration began negotiating with a consortium of gun manufacturers in an attempt to get the gun makers to accept a "best practices" code of behavior that the government believed would limit gun trafficking and thus reduce gun deaths. Basically, the gun manufacturers were asked to be responsible not only for how they sold guns to wholesalers, which accounted for at least 90% of their sales, but also for the manner in which wholesalers sold to retailers and how retailers sold to their storefront customers.

The negotiations dragged on for several years and, Department of Justice PR to the contrary, the plan was both unfeasible and unworkable. To begin, Smith & Wesson sold almost all its production to some 30-odd national wholesalers, but these companies in turn shipped product to several thousand retailers. And at one point during the negotiations, S&W did a survey of their dealers to discover, much to their surprise, that less than 25% of all their guns were being sold by medium and large shops and the great bulk of their guns were ending up with dealers who were selling less than 50 of their guns a year.

81

Additionally, many Smith & Wesson dealers did not have retail storefronts, particularly in Southern states where zoning and other commercial ordnances were thin or non-existent. Finally, a large proportion of the factory's annual production, upwards of 25%, were being sold at pawn shops who held FFL's to sell guns but were basically in the business of receiving and re-selling the usual pawn merchandise: watches, jewelry, television sets and broken guitars. To impose a code of best practices on such a disparate group of retailers was one thing; to enforce it was another. Neither was very practical and, at the very least, they would result in increased distribution costs and diminished sales (which was the DOJ's intent in the first place).

At the same time that these talks were taking place, a series of class-action lawsuits against gun makers were also slowly wending their way through the federal judicial system. Many of these suits were the handiwork of law firms that specialized in class-action torts and had come up short in legal battles against the cigarette industry. But other suits reflected the concerns of civil rights and social advocacy groups, many of whom were trying to develop a strategy to cope with the alarming rise in inner-city gun violence that began to occur during the first Clinton administration.

In the early 60s, homicides each year counted less than 10,000, but this number began to increase to the point where more than 20,000 Americans were murdered each year beginning in the mid-80's, a number which continued to creep upwards into the 1990's. Much of this violence was the handiwork of drug dealers, and still more reflected the ongoing turf battles of inner-city gangs. But either way, most of these deadly assaults were taking place in black, inner-city neighborhoods where a high level of gun deaths in almost every city was coterminous with a proliferation of guns.

I will talk a little further about the political and judicial reaction to these lawsuits but the bottom line was that the gun industry, having failed to halt an assault weapons ban in 1994, felt increasingly vulnerable to the possibility that, at some point, a series of class-action suits would either harm them irreparably or weigh them down with massive legal costs. Nevertheless, from the mid-90's until the end of 1999, the gun industry stuck together and whether they were negotiating in good or bad faith was no matter, the bottom line was that they continued to resist a government deal which, in return for agreeing to some best practice distribution code, would have required the government to immunize them from the various class-action suits.

In March, 2000, a bombshell hit the gun industry when Smith & Wesson and the Department of Justice jointly announced that they had concluded secret negotiations and that America's second-oldest gun company (after Colt) was going to sign an agreement that would protect them from class-action federal suits. Although both sides claimed that Smith & Wesson's decision would protect all the gun manufacturers from legal challenges to their business activity, it wasn't really clear that this was the case. Word also leaked out that another party to the talks—Glock—had walked away from the table because they didn't think the manufacturers were getting a good deal. Part of the problem on both sides was the uncertainty over the forthcoming presidential election, in which it was assumed that a continuation of the White House in Democratic hands would mean an even more forceful anti-gun approach on the part of the DOJ. And thrown into the mix was the fact that a special DOJ Task Force was also beginning to work on the first national gun violence program that would link more aggressive policing efforts at the local level to more aggressive enforcement of gun laws by the ATF.

Within 24 hours after S&W and the DOJ went public with their deal, the gun world, led by the NRA, struck back. S&W was denounced as a "traitor," a "turncoat," a "bloodsucking parasite," and those were some of the more polite comments. As more details of the agreement came out, several distributors cancelled orders, dealers took down S&W banners and removed guns from their shelves, and there were even rumors that shooters were coming by the factory on Roosevelt Avenue in Springfield to discard guns in the guard house at the front gate. Much of this activity was orchestrated and led by the NRA, which praised the other gun makers for steadfastly resisting the government's pressure, while excoriating S&W for caving in on the deal.

Smith & Wesson was not only a storied brand in the American gun industry, its history was intertwined with the city of Springfield and the whole development and history of Gun Valley. The original factory was located on

Stockbridge Street in downtown Springfield, just six blocks from City Hall and less than a quarter mile from the east bank of the Connecticut River. Just up the hill from the four-story, L-shaped, red-brick factory was the largest private home in Springfield built by the company's co-founder, Daniel Baird Wesson. He had started as a gun engineer at the Springfield Arsenal but left in 1856 to set up his own company, and the onset of the Civil War and consequent demand for his Model 2 revolver made "DB" the wealthiest resident of the city. It was said that he built his mansion to impress his father-in-law who was angered when he learned of the prospective marriage of his daughter to Wesson, telling friends that "my daughter isn't going to marry a gun smith."

S&W Stockbridge Street factory

In addition to the regal residence, Wesson also later built the hospital, known as Wesson Memorial Hospital, which stands further up the same hill and across the street from the Arsenal. It's worth mentioning, incidentally, that the front of the hospital, which still contains the modern outpatient pediatric clinic, faces one of the most famous streets in all of the United States, which happens to be named Mulberry Street—yes, of Dr. Seuss fame.

The factory down at the bottom of the hill anchored the South end of Springfield and gave the downtown much of its personality and luster, until it was closed when the company moved out to its present-day location in a neighborhood known as Indian Orchard on the eastern edge of the city. In the 1960's probably 95% of all handguns carried by American cops were S&W K-frame revolvers, of which the initial model had first gone into production in 1899. And even though the company had suffered through some missteps in recent years, including not moving from revolvers to pistols in the face of European competitors like Sig, Beretta and Glock, there was still no American gun manufacturer, not even Colt, Ruger, Remington or Winchester, whose brand name and logo were as synonymous with the small arms industry located in Gun Valley.

All of that history, tradition and goodwill very quickly collapsed once the NRA decided that S&W's deal with the Clinton Administration was an insult to gun owners and a threat to the industry. "Those were the black days at 2100," a senior S&W product manager once told me, referring to the company's address on Roosevelt Avenue. "We came to work every day not knowing if the plant would be open or shut." For over a year the company teetered on the edge of bankruptcy, with sales dropping almost in half, and most of the factory production lines shut down. At one point the company workforce that had numbered almost 2,000 in the mid-80's was reduced to half that number, and the plant in Houlton, Maine, which made the handcuffs and the .22 pistols, was shuttered entirely.

What saved Smith & Wesson from oblivion the following year was not the company's sale to a new investor group that publicly disavowed the government deal, but rather the election of George W. Bush, whose administration let it be known that they weren't eager to pursue the issue any further. It's too early to make historical judgments about events that occurred just a few short years ago, but one could probably argue that Bush's presidency may have been the most gun-friendly administration that the gun industry and its supporters and followers have ever known. Most important was the 2005 Protection of Lawful Commerce in Arms Act, which immunized gun manufacturers from the class-action suits that had been rumbling around since the mid-90's, the threat of which had driven Smith & Wesson to make their "devil's deal" with the Clinton Administration in 2000. Basically, the law halted in its tracks many of the federal class-action suits that threatened the industry, as well as a number of suits brought by municipalities against gun makers for allegedly flooding urban areas with too many guns. The law required that every new handgun be shipped from the factory with a locking device, but also granted civil immunity to gun owners whose guns were used in crimes, provided they could prove that their gun was inoperable at the time it was taken from their control.

In 2003 the Bush Administration also agreed to an annual rider to the ATF funding bill known as the Tiahrt Amendment, which tightened controls around data generated by NICS background checks. The Amendment, strongly backed by the NRA, made it more difficult to access the trace information database and also strengthened the procedures that required NICS to destroy data connected to all positive background checks within 24 hours after the check was carried out. Neither of these laws had a major impact on either the background check system, nor on the degree to which law enforcement could use the NICS system to track illegal guns. But like the 2005 law that immunized the gun industry from class-action suits, these actions sent a message to gun owners that the NRA was their champion when it came to protecting them from efforts to make the purchase or ownership of guns more legally onerous.

This brings us to the high-point of the NRA's political crusade over the past twenty years, namely, the 2008 SCOTUS 2nd Amendment decision that affirmed the private ownership of guns as a basic constitutional right. Enough has been written and spoken about this decision that I feel confident simply noting some of the other sources and assuming that you will refer or not refer to them as the case might be. But there are two parts of the decision which need to be briefly mentioned within the context of this chapter and its focus on the activities and strategies of the NRA. First, while the decision which affirmed the 2nd Amendment as a fundamental constitutional guarantee put an end to a legal debate that had been dragging on since at least the ambiguous *Miller* decision handed down in 1939, the Court made it clear that the right to own or possess a firearm was limited only to guns kept in the home, regardless of the purpose of ownership or the status of the owner.

The debate over the meaning of the phrase "keep and bear arms" had nothing to do with the government's authority to create military or quasi-military forces to prepare for the "common defense." It had to do with whether an individual had to be enrolled or otherwise connected to some government-led military force in order to keep a gun at home. And on this point the Court definitively declared that the intention of the Framers was to allow citizens to possess and keep a firearm in their residence in order to defend themselves, regardless of any commitment to being called to join any government military force or organization of any kind.

The majority decision ratifying the fundamental right to self-defense through ownership of a firearm also contained some significant limitations, none of which seem to ever get into the gun control debate from either side. First, Justice Scalia (who wrote the majority decision) explicitly noted that, like the 1st Amendment's protection of freedom of speech, the 2nd Amendment did not confer unlimited rights to the use of a gun. Second, Scalia specifically noted that the ownership, possession and use of a handgun for self-defense was based on the right to keep a gun "in the home." Finally and most important, the majority decision did not foreclose the right of government to enact and enforce gun control laws, including "laws imposing conditions and qualifications on the commercial sale of arms."

Perhaps the public relations team that works for the NRA hasn't bothered to read Scalia's decision, or better yet probably knows that nobody else has read it either, but the bottom line is that the NRA's strategy and message about gun ownership since the 2008 *District of Columbia v. Heller* decision has been to assume that any attempt to impose even the slightest condition or regulation on firearms ownership or use is an attack on gun owners' 2nd Amendment rights.

The NRA has used the 2nd Amendment "threat" to great advantage since 2008, particularly in its efforts to widen the acceptability of concealed carry permits and weaken or oppose other gun control laws in general. This was particularly the case in states which attempted to impose new restrictions in the wake of the December, 2012 Sandy Hook massacre, when more restrictive gun laws were passed in Colorado, New York and Connecticut, that in every case imposed magazine capacity limitations for semi-automatic rifles. Similar restrictions were introduced in other states but largely went nowhere due to NRA opposition based on preserving 2nd Amendment ownership rights.

The single most extreme instance in which the NRA and its allies attempted to widen the regulatory borders by citing constitutional protections, however, occurred in Florida when a law was passed by the legislature and then signed by Governor Rick Scott that criminalized any attempt by a physician to talk to a patient about the existence of guns in the home. The law took effect in 2011 but was immediately and ultimately permanently delayed by a Federal judge who cited the 1st Amendment rights of physicians to inquire about other safety issues like tobacco, drugs, seat belts and backyard swimming pools.

The decision, which has been appealed by the State of Florida, not only cited the long-standing "right to know" of medical practice, but also scored the NRA and other sponsors of the law for relying on unsubstantiated anecdotes rather than any empirical evidence when they claimed that such doctor-patient discussion could lead to disclosures that might result in the confiscation of guns. In Chapter 4 we will examine how the NRA and its academic research supporters often present anecdotal information as scientifically derived data, but in this instance the motivation behind this law (and similar laws in other states, none of which were implemented) was the result of a long-running argument between pro-gun advocates and physicians about the health impact of guns.

Beginning in the late 1980's, the Centers for Disease Control began to list gun homicides not only as a specific category of morbidity but as a concern for public health. This led to the funding of some CDC-sponsored research on gun violence, which then led to findings about the relationship between the existence of guns and certain types of health issues (suicide in particular) that were used by gun control advocates in the run-up to the assault weapons ban enacted in 1994. Two years later the NRA convinced Congress that CDC-financed gun research was unreliable and biased against gun owners, with the result that legislation was passed which permanently prohibited the CDC from budgeting or awarding funds for any research about guns.

Nevertheless, the acrimony between medical associations and the NRA continued, and became particularly noisy in the wake of Aurora, Sandy Hook and the attempt in April, 2013 to pass a new federal gun control bill. Some of the NRA's anger at physicians, particularly pediatricians and family health providers, was simply due to the fact that, generally speaking, physicians tend not to be gun owners and are therefore no friends of the NRA. But part of the antipathy towards physicians is also a reflection of the larger strategy to make guns as acceptable as possible in order to strengthen the market for commercial sales. In Chapter 4 I'll discuss this issue in detail. Let's just say at this point that the 2nd Amendment rights affirmed by the 2008 decision have sometimes mattered and sometimes not.

Like the battles over the 2nd Amendment, the result of the NRA's and its allies' political spending has also been mixed. Between 2000 and 2010, pro-gun money going to congressional races totaled 28 times as much money as what was given out by gun control groups, with the pro-gun contributions at $7 million and the gun control money less than 250 grand. This disparity is enormous, but as a percentage of campaign contributions flowing into those five election cycles, it's a tiny drop in a very large bucket. To elect one President, 33 senators and 435 representatives in 2012 we spent around $7 billion. So all the money that the gun lobby poured into campaigns between 2000 and 2010 equaled about 1/1000th of what the 2012 campaign cost alone. Furthermore, if you look at the spread of pro-gun donations to individual races, you quickly discover that most of the money is spent in places where the differences between the candidates on gun issues is usually much less than what exists between senators and representatives who come from pro-gun, as opposed to anti-gun states or districts. The ten largest recipients of pro-gun money in Congress since 2000 all come from either Western or Southern states where it's assumed and usually true that everyone running for office is more or less pro-gun. Voting the NRA position on guns in a state like Oklahoma is about as much a test of the strength of a politician's backbone as being pro-Israel if you represent New York City or Miami Beach.

The bottom line on the strength and power of the NRA is that it's a mixed bag. They have won some important victories over the last twenty years, they have also seen gun control advanced, particularly in some places where horrendous acts of gun violence have occurred. What makes them the central player in the national discussion about guns is that they are always more concerned about connecting to gun owners than they are concerned about connecting with the other side. And in this respect they understand the hopes, expectations and anger of their constituency very well. But the way they play to the mentality of gun owners, while being their greatest strength, is also their greatest weakness when it comes to reaching out beyond their core support. Because what the NRA has not been able to do is convince anyone who doesn't own a gun that the 2nd Amendment is some kind of sacred trust. To be sure, the platitudes and bromides about "respecting gun owner's rights" are the preface to any gun control speech uttered by President Obama on down. But nobody's really kidding anyone else in this regard. If you're not a gun owner and the guns disappeared, you wouldn't miss them at all, not one bit.

CHAPTER 3

WANT TO MAKE A MILLION DOLLARS IN THE GUN BUSINESS?

You'll have to get to the last sentence of this chapter to learn the answer to that question, but I guarantee you there's one very easy way to do it. Only before looking at the answer, you should spend some time reading the text that follows because I'm going to explain the economics of the gun business and show you why making a pile of dough in this business isn't the easiest thing to do.

The first and most difficult problem encountered by people who make or sell guns is that it's the one consumer item that simply doesn't get used up or worn out. There's a reason why most Americans spend the bulk of their weekly earnings on food, clothing and gasoline; they have to replace those items almost every day. The folks who analyze the gun business estimate that there are probably around 5,000 retail storefronts engaged in the retail sale of guns. There are more than 120,000 gasoline stations and nearly 100,000 of them are also convenience stores selling all that luscious junk food that we can't do without. That's what happens when you sell something that everyone wants and wants again and again. That's not guns.

95

I own a commercial model of the Colt Army 45 pistol that was manufactured in 1919. Other than the magazine, which appears to be the same vintage although it may or may not be the magazine that originally shipped from the factory along with the gun, every part is original and the finish has never been redone or retouched in any way. I have also shot this gun at least 1,000 times and I have no idea how much the gun was shot before I bought it in 1989. So here's a cheap consumer product that is almost a century old and still works the way it worked when it came off the factory line. This gun may be a somewhat extreme example of how long guns last, but it's hardly the only century-old working handgun that I've seen.

Part of the problem involved in the lack of obsolescence is the fact that the technology behind how small arms functions hasn't really changed since smokeless gun powder was adapted for rifle and then handgun cartridges beginning in 1875. Smokeless powder was much less powerful than black powder which was used in flintlock rifles (and is still used in fireworks), but it ignited much more quickly and also produced less powder fouling which made it a more efficient propellant for fast-loading semi-automatic and fully automatic guns. Like many small arms technologies, the initial developments took place in Europe and led to the growth of the great fortune of Alfred Nobel. But once the technology came across the Atlantic it was immediately adapted by the small arms industry and led not only to the appearance of mass-produced small arms ammunition by companies like

DuPont, but also sparked the growth of more firearms manufacturers in and around the Connecticut River Valley.

The one major firearms manufacturer that did not first appear in Gun Valley was Remington, which was founded in Ilion, New York, on the banks of the Mohawk River, in 1816. An attempt to supplement arms manufacture with typewriters didn't work out and that part of the business, known as Remington-Rand, was spun off in 1886. Ironically, the Remington-Rand Corp. would return to gun making during World War II, when the government took over the facility and used it to produce more than 1 million Colt 1911A1 Army pistols between 1943 and 1945. The Ilion plant also was converted to military production during the war and manufactured the bolt-action Enfield rifle that was carried by U.S. troops until the semi-automatic Garand came on-line at the end of 1943.

Remington factory, Ilion, NY, undated

Remington was not only the oldest, continually operating gun manufacturer in the United States, it was also another iconic brand name throughout the world, both in guns and ammunition. The only problem is that the success of the brand never translated into success on the balance sheet. Despite making and selling millions of Model 700 bolt-action hunting rifles and millions more

Model 1100 semi-automatic shotguns, the company teetered on the brink of insolvency decade after decade, and when the most recent owners acquired Remington in 2007, they took possession of an old, red-brick factory in Ilion, New York along with nearly 300 million dollars in debt.

The financial fortunes of the other great brand names in the firearms business weren't much better. Even before the 2000 NRA-led boycott, Smith & Wesson had been teetering along since the mid-90's when it began to lose its long-dominated police business to the European pistol-makers like Glock and Sig. In fact, even the Massachusetts State Police in Smith & Wesson's home state had chosen to replace their old Smith & Wesson duty revolvers with the Sig 226 pistol. As for the most famous American gun maker, Colt, their management had moved production out of the brick factory on the banks of the Connecticut River in Hartford, sold off the military rifle business to a separate investment group and reduced its commercial handgun catalog to a few revolvers that nobody wanted and a civilian version of the 1911 Army pistol whose design was now copied and outsold by other manufacturers, chief among them Kimber Arms.

Even the Springfield Armory, where the entire small arms industry first started, has not been immune to the pressures that keep guns on the margin of profitability and financial health. Production at the armory in Springfield ended in 1968 and most of the facility now houses a technical-vocational college (along with a very nice museum run by the National Parks Service). The name, however, was ultimately revived in 1974 by a private arms maker who continues to make a civilian version of the M-14 rifle (the successor to the M-1 Garand) and various copies of the 1911 Army pistol at a plant in Geneseo, Illinois. What the new company is really known for, however, is its line of polymer XD pistols which are manufactured in Croatia but proudly bear the Springfield Armory name and logo on every frame and slide. Want to be a player in the U.S. gun business? Take an iconic name and outsource the production overseas.

The fact that firearms sales over the last several years have exceeded all expectations should not make anyone think that all of a sudden there's lots of money to be made in guns. To begin with, supply and demand in this industry is not driven by market forces but rather reflects the volatility of the political environment in which guns are regulated and discussed. Demand for guns and ammunition is also largely conditioned on the perception of gun owners about whether their ability to purchase or own guns is threatened either because of a horrendous event (Columbine, Aurora, Sandy Hook, et. al.), or because an anti-gun politician shows up at 1600 Pennsylvania Avenue in Washington, D.C. Finally, gun sales may also be affected by general or specific concerns about lawlessness, mass violence ("terrorism" in its modern form) or socio-economic threats. Let's look at each of these market-influencing factors in turn.

Generally speaking, Democrats in power tends to help gun sales, Republicans in power tends to hurt. Part of this blue—bad, red—good syllogism stems from the fact that gun culture is much more firmly rooted in red states for reasons having to do with the country's history, as I explained in Chapter 1. But it also has to do with the ideological messaging of both parties and the degree to which they differ over government regulation, not just over guns but over social issues in general. The problem is that major electoral shifts occur in the U.S. with great frequency, which means that every two years the gun industry faces the uncertainty of a political realignment that can dramatically influence market penetration and sales. Because the fact is that, no matter how you cut it, experience tells us that whenever the government regulates anything, either the price goes up or the supply goes down, or both. And since government regulation of guns, by definition, always centers on the idea of making it more difficult for people to own them, the gun industry is always one step away from feeling that it is about to be shut down.

If the industry isn't going to be shut down by regulations, then it's going to find itself facing diminishing sales if the regulators lose the election and are replaced by the non-regulators whose assumption of political and regulatory power makes gun consumers feel that they can put off buying that next gun because they'll always be able to find it on the retail shelves. For example, from mid-Summer, 2008 until November, 2010, gun and ammunition sales soared due to the imminent and then ultimate electoral victory of Barack Obama, who was rightfully pictured by the gun industry as their greatest-ever threat. This anti-gun image of Obama was not just based on his background, liberal policies and uber-regulatory instincts, it was most of all a reflection of deep-seated fear and resentment of an *activist* black politician that was a fundamental slice of the world view in areas of the South and Midwest where gun ownership was always strongest and conservative ideology the most extreme.

But guess what happened after the Tea Party victories and the change from Democratic to Republican majorities in the House of Representatives following the election of 2010? If you were a gun retailer like me you couldn't give away your inventory. If you were a wholesaler, all of a sudden you began to announce specials and promotions. And if you were a manufacturer, you thanked God that the demand for guns over the previous couple of years hadn't tricked you into investing in expensive new equipment to increase manufacturing capacity to meet what turned out to look like just a brief, two-year surge in demand.

The 2010 election wasn't the first time in recent memory that the gun business suddenly spiked upwards and then, just as quickly, slowed back down. Within 48 hours after the 9-11 attacks, gun shops all over the country were reporting a mad rush for guns and ammunition which they were not able to meet, particularly because September is traditionally the beginning of the hunting season so retail inventories were loaded up with hunting rifles and shotguns, whereas the generalized fears created by bin Laden's little air force squadron prompted people to look for self-defense weapons, in particular tactical-style shotguns and handguns. By the time manufacturers were able to re-set production and move inventory to the wholesalers, demand had already started to level off and within 60 days of the World Trade Center and Pentagon attacks, most parts of the country were not seeing any more demand beyond the normal increases that usually occurred in gun sales between Labor Day and the end of the calendar year. By the summer of 2002, gun sales had slipped down to below levels registered during the summer of 2001.

The middle tier between the factories and the retailers is occupied by three groups who between them account for the sales of virtually the entire production of the major gun companies and probably more than 70% of all the guns sold in the United States each year. In addition to the wholesalers, which is one group, there are also some chain stores, like Cabela's, Gander Mountain, Dunham's and Big 5 Sports, which is the second group, and then the third group which is four or five hundred of the larger retailers who belong to national dealer co-ops, like Sports, Inc., and Nation's Best Sports. The chain stores and the dealer co-ops probably account for another 15-20% of gun distribution and the final chunk, counting at best 10% of all guns sold each year, come from smaller manufacturers and importers who sell directly to dealers or consumers for the most part through internet channels.

The distribution of ammunition tends to parallel the distribution of firearms but if anything is more concentrated in the distributor channel, because very few retail stores have either the room or the financial resources to purchase ammunition in large enough quantities to make the shipping costs of this heavy item viable.

Wholesalers have warehouses where they can store millions of cartridges, dealers have a few shelves that can hold a box of this and a box of that. The problem with ammunition is that when you get past the common calibers like 22, 38, 357 or 9mm, it's impossible to stock all the other calibers or the different variations within a particular caliber, so the retailer splits the margin with his wholesalers but doesn't assume the cost of storing or carrying the lesser-requested ammunition on his own shelves.

When it comes to accessories—holsters, optics and the like—the distribution tends to be wider and increasingly dominated by the web if only because interstate shipment of guns and ammunition requires federal licensing whereas everything else is no different from any other consumer product. While a certain degree of accessory sales therefore disappear from the manufacturer wholesale retail network, gun revenues account for at least 80% of all sales at the retail level, and this is true for the wholesale, chain store and co-op markets as well. Outside of the major chain stores, very few retailers carry any inventory beyond either guns and related products or guns, fishing and related products. The term "outdoor sports" has traditionally covered hunting and fishing, but both of these activities have experienced slower growth over the last several decades than the newer outdoor activities, like biking, trekking, climbing, camping and other active outdoor sports. The largest, mega-mall sporting goods stores like Cabela's and Bass Pro cater to both types of consumers, but virtually every college town in America has a nice shop where you can buy a tent, a mountain bike or an expensive pair of hiking shoes. I don't remember the last time I saw a gun shop within the proximity of a college campus.

Now on to the finances of the gun business. The good news about the gun business at the manufacturer and wholesale levels is that it tends to have a fairly steady and predictable cash flow. The bad news is that the margins are pretty crummy. This has to do with a number of factors, chief among them the basic reality of the gun business, namely, that while demand for guns is sometimes quite elastic, particularly when an exceptional circumstance like the election of an extremely liberal, black activist President spurs fears of new barriers to gun ownership, the number of customers is quite inelastic. Despite the degree to which Smith & Wesson, Colt and Winchester are iconic names known and recognized by virtually everyone in the United States, there has been no real change in the percentage of Americans who actually own guns (or at least admit to legal gun possession) and even with the recent, Obama-inspired surge in retail sales, the percentage of American homes that contain guns may actually be even less than it was previously.

Not only are the number of gun consumers stagnant, but even within this population the majority of guns are owned by hobbyists who make most of their gun purchases on impulse. And impulse shopping has a funny way of being both unpredictable and subject to all kinds of factors that may or may not lead to a purchase of any particular item at all. Even the most hard-core gun owner will put off a purchase if the family budget might be stretched too thin, and many guns that are bought on impulse get offered back to the dealer for repurchase if a more necessary expenditure—tires or brakes being frequently mentioned—needs to take place. For these reasons, gun prices tend to remain stable even during periods when they are hard to find. At the beginning of 2013 when a new gun control was being debated after the massacre at Sandy Hook, most major gun manufacturers were reporting that they had booked orders that could not be filled for 6 to 9 months. Meanwhile, gun prices at the wholesale and retail levels hardly moved upwards at all.

Generally speaking, the gross margin from factory to retail counter in the gun business averages about 40%. Depending on the particular product, most retailers operate on 20-25% margin for new guns, and if they are lucky can get a bit wider margin for accessories and ammunition. But since gun sales usually represent 80% of the overall retail revenue or higher, gun shops aren't for the most part very profitable ventures. The chain stores and dealer co-ops make out better because they purchase inventory in large enough volume to go outside the reliance on wholesalers and thus pick up the additional 12-15% that otherwise would revert to the middle tier. But for every chain store like Dick's, Cabela's or Dunham's, there are 40-50 smaller retailers who, in the aggregate, sell the bulk of the guns. And most of these stores are owned by the same kind of people who come in as customers; they are gun hobbyists who are often retired from some blue-collar gig and derive enough income independent of their store to become an even more active hobbyist than they were before.

As for the gun wholesalers, their continued existence is largely predicated on the fact that, unlike other consumer durables, in particular tools and hardware that have succumbed to the discount chains' economies of scale, retail gun shops represent virtually the last bastion of consumer activity that still takes place in individual, independently owned stores. But since the wholesalers are all selling exactly the same products to retailers who are carrying inventories comprised of items that nobody really *needs*, the same downward pressures that are exerted at the retail sales counter are felt by the wholesale telemarketer as well. Like the retailers, there are a few large wholesale houses whose total staffs number in the several hundreds and who have gross revenues of $500 million or more. But many of the 30-odd national gun wholesalers have total annual revenue under $200 million, which isn't something to sneeze at but also not a very big deal. My father managed a family-owned dairy in central New Jersey and their annual sales in the 1980's were about $400 million a year. His outfit sold milk to school kids and housewives and had greater yearly sales than all but two or three of the largest gun wholesalers. In fact, his dairy in those years had higher annual revenues than Smith & Wesson, and as I used to joke with him, it wasn't like his dairy had any kind of worldwide, iconic name.

The great John Browning. He was to gun design what Einstein was to physics. Made it understandable.

To counter the tendency for gun sales and revenues to slowly slide downhill, gun manufacturers go to great lengths to make up for a contracting market by introducing an endless list of new products. But the new products don't in any way change the technology or basic design of guns. And whether it's a little, single-shot 22 rifle that used to be put under the Christmas tree, or a 90 millimeter howitzer that can lob a 12-pound shell a mile or more, all guns work basically the same way: the bullet leaves the cartridge casing because the powder inside the case ignites, changing from a solid to a gas, and the gas needs to expand which it does by pushing the bullet out of the shell. The whole point of the barrel is to force the bullet to fly off in a specific direction, the whole point of the hammer and trigger is to create the impact against the chemical inside the shell to create the spark which detonates the powder and off we go. The force of the gas escaping from the case behind the bullet can also be used to re-load the gun for the next shot depending on the design of the weapon, a technology first discovered by John Browning in 1905. To show you what he a genius he was, Browning figured this out while walking through a field and noticing how the wind scattered dandelion plants that had just bloomed.

Colt 45 Pistol – Browning design not changed since 1907

There have been many changes in the look and feel of guns over the subsequent century, but they are all cosmetic in the sense that guns still work the same way today that they did back then. The manufacturers use different materials, the guns are coated with different finishes, every once in a while the industry comes out with a new caliber. But like internal-combustion engines that power automobiles, changes in models reflect changes in manufacturing techniques and consumer taste, they don't really change the basic way that cars or guns work. So the challenge in the gun industry is two-fold: first, you have to find new customers who can be persuaded to buy their first and then subsequent guns; second, to get the hobbyists who own the overwhelming majority of guns to keep coming back to expand their collections by buying more guns. In both respects, the industry has been in the recent short-term moderately successful, but nobody in the gun business is kidding anyone that the long-term business prospects are all that bright.

As to finding new customers, the industry has focused its efforts on two of the groups that traditionally were outside the usual demographic pattern that defined gun ownership: women and kids, the latter either as gun owners if over the age of 21, or as shooters who would eventually gravitate to becoming gun owners once they came of age. For women, acceptance of guns in the home was a given for those who were married to male shooters. Most female spouses of gun owners, particularly the hobbyists, come from the same social background, usually possess a little bit but not a lot more education, and often come out of homes where guns were owned by siblings or parents. So being around guns and being comfortable with guns was and is not unusual for this demographic group. Owning a gun, on the other hand, presumes that whether the gun is used for self-defense or reflects an interest in pursuing guns as a hobby, these women feel a perceived need to purchase and own guns. And that is generally speaking not true.

On the other hand, if the traditional gun-owning demographic (white male, 40+, blue collar) is slowly eroding, the number of women who are single parents or living outside of standard, heterosexual matrimony is steadily increasing. And the industry, both the manufacturers and the advocacy allies, have been promoting female gun ownership in particular aimed (pardon the pun) at single women who, by dint of domestic circumstances, might feel more inclined to be concerned about self-protection and home defense. The problem is, however, that no matter how you dress up a gun so that it might appeal to a woman, such as with a more artistic finish, or pink grips, or held by a designer-style holster that fits cutely inside the purse, women, generally speaking, tend to be much more averse to the use of violence than men. And since hunting never engaged women to any great degree and as an outdoor activity is falling off anyway, the only rationale for female gun ownership is personal security and protection, for which most women just don't want to use guns.

The second major group that gun makers are trying to lure into the retail environment are younger men, under the age of thirty, who traditionally had no interest in guns. Much of the interest of the pre-thirty age group in small arms stems from the cycling through Iraq and Afghanistan of several million soldiers since the Taliban regime was toppled in Afghanistan in 2002. All of these soldiers are volunteers, and many join because the financial enlistment bonuses, salaries and hazardous combat-zone pay go far beyond anything that they could earn back home, which means they have plenty of money with which to purchase more expensive toys. This may seem rather difficult to believe, given the horrendous stories that we hear every day about the effect of both physical and mental battle injuries on the lives of veterans when they return home, but most of our military in battle zones are there because they want to be there and they enjoy both the risks and rewards of their duty overseas.

One of the attractions of active combat duty is the degree to which our troops can supply themselves with customized gear, and transition from being a video gamer to the real thing. Battle rifles are issued by and returned to the military because nobody is going back into civilian life with a machine gun strapped to his waist. But optics are often purchased in retail stores at home or over the internet, ditto knives and other assorted military gear. Other than weapons, the only real difference between how the troops are outfitted as opposed to the private mercenaries both from America and overseas, is that the latter usually also purchase their own uniforms, whereas the U.S. military troops are issued battle fatigues and other clothing, whether they choose to wear it or not.

The point is that the young men and women who come home from combat zones didn't give up a year or two years of civilian life unwillingly and are therefore anxious to put it all behind them and reactivate the lives they led before they were sent abroad. They chose to enter the military as a job, they earned good money while they were working, and at the end of their tour they often came home for a brief respite before they chose to go off and fight again. Today's military isn't like the old days when we had a large "wartime" force in which everyone participated and many fought, versus a "peacetime" force in which few served and nobody fought. The country and society in general has become much more militarized; troops are now lionized as "warriors," and the notion of a distinction between a nation "at war" and a nation "at peace" has disappeared.

The gun industry has jumped all over this new, pro-military culture in its rush to manufacture and distribute what those of us in the business refer to as "black" guns. What are black guns? It's the finish that is painted on military-style rifles, aka "assault" rifles, whose sales have been a significant part of the recent surge of gun ownership, in particular since 2008. Note to the hard-core readers: don't start jumping up and down because I used the word "assault" to describe a semi-automatic gun. I'm going to talk about this issue in detail because, in many respects, the arguments over assault-style weapons and gun magazine capacities have been central to the pro-gun and anti-gun positions that underlie the whole debate. Pardon the pun, but hold your fire.

To begin, you have to understand the place of military arms in the gun-owners lexicon and arsenals. If you want to believe the gun folks today, military arms were used by civilians and were known as "modern sporting rifles" from sometime during the last century. The National Shooting Sports Foundation (NSSF) claims that MSRs were the lever-action rifles developed by Spencer and later by Winchester with a tubular magazine that held 8-10 rounds. The rifles were shorter and lighter than standard infantry guns and were used primarily by cavalry units. The Winchester repeater saw more frequent use during the two decades it took to pacify the various Plains Indian tribes, and from that time until the present continues to be favored by hunters primarily for short-distance deer shoots.

There's only one problem with this little NSSF history lesson: the term "Modern Sporting Rifle" didn't exist back when Spencer and Winchester made their rifles. The term was coined, in fact, by the NSSF and the gun industry to get such products accepted by chain stores like Cabela's that were at first reluctant to display military-style weapons in retail venues frequented by families (read: mothers and children). The gun industry portrays the design of these rifles as nothing more than just another example of consumer goods reflecting changing tastes, as in the following quote by NSSF President Steve Sanetti: "Nothing looks like it did 50 or 100 years ago. Today, this is the way a rifle looks. It doesn't have a wood stock or blued steel. Yet it has become 'America's rifle.'"

But hold on a minute, Steve. There are many rifles out there today that look *exactly* like they looked fifty years ago. The semi-auto Remington 759, still a very popular gun, has been in production (with various name changes) since 1952. The Browning BAR, another semi-auto hunting rifle, basically hasn't changed since 1967. What's changed is the gun industry's attempt to make high-capacity, military-style rifles palatable with today's political sensitivities, not today's marketing tastes. When I bought my first Colt AR-15 *thirty-five years ago*, nobody had any problem referring to it as an assault rifle. The term had been around since the end of World War II, when it first was applied to an automatic rifle, the StG 44, known as the *sturmgewehr* (which literally means "assault" or "storm") issued to units of the Wehrmacht in 1944.

The landscape began to change in 1994, when the Democrats, led by Dianne Feinstein, pushed through a ten-year ban on "assault" rifles as part of a national anti-crime bill. According to the NSSF and other gun industry mouthpieces, the use of the term "assault rifle" was an attempt by anti-gun elements to get rid of these weapons by creating the fiction that they were no different from rifles used by the military. In fact, it wasn't only liberal, anti-gun "elements" that ganged up on the poor, law-abiding assault rifle owners. On the eve of the vote in Congress, the following letter was sent to Republican congressmen, urging them to vote for the ban: "As a longtime gun owner and supporter of the right to bear arms, I, too, have carefully thought about this issue. I am convinced that the limitations imposed in this bill are absolutely necessary. I know there is heavy pressure on you to go the other way, but I strongly urge you to join me in supporting this bill. It must be passed." The author of the letter, a really hard-core member of the liberal "element," was Ronald Reagan.

The NSSF can say whatever it wants about why the Modern Sporting Rifle is different from military weapons, but the difference boils down to one thing, namely, that assault rifles used by the military are designed to shoot multiple rounds with one pull of the trigger (automatic) while the civilian versions require a separate trigger pull (semi-automatic) for every shot. But from a design and function perspective, this is hardly a game-changer, because most assault weapons carried today by the military also provide the option of being fired on either automatic or semi-automatic mode. In fact, most assault weapons carried by our guys and gals in combat zones shoot either one or two shots for each trigger pull, because the odds of putting more than two auto-fire shots on target are slim to none.

If anyone out there really believes that the purpose of making a civilian version of the assault rifle is to somehow lull consumers into thinking that they aren't getting their hands on a military gun, consider the description of the product by Colt Firearms, the company that manufactured both the first military and civilian versions: "Colt's rifles are the only rifles available to sportsmen, hunters and other shooters that are manufactured in the Colt factory and based on the same military standards and specifications as the United States issue Colt M16 rifle and M4 carbine."

Here's the real irony about assault rifles as consumer products: the gun was originally designed by a brilliant firearms engineer named Gene Stoner who was working for a division of ArmaLite, then known as the Fairchild Corporation. The whole point of ArmaLite was to manufacture military small arms using lightweight materials (hence the company name), because everyone who had served in World War II, including Stoner, could never forget lugging that ten-pound rifle all over the battlefields of Western Europe and the Pacific. Unfortunately, the Fairchild Corporation always teetered on the brink of financial collapse, and when the ArmaLite Division was sold to a group of private investors, a group that included Stoner, they didn't have much money either. Finally, the gun's design was so radically different from the gun it would replace—the M14—that the Army took its sweet time deciding whether or not to adopt a new gun at all.

Gene Stoner – the most original American gun designer since John Browning

To make a very long story short, eventually Stoner and his buddies ran out of money and sold the design to Colt Firearms whose engineers first converted it into a semi-automatic rifle, the AR-15, for civilian sales and then, several years later, offered a fully automatic version known as the M-16 to the U.S. government for military use. That's right, folks. The current Colt M4 rifle carried by our troops (and plenty of other combatants) started out as a *commercial* design that was redesigned for military use—not the other way around. Oh well, why let a few facts stand in the way of strongly held opinions? I bought my first Colt AR-15 in 1977; the real truth is that I traded a Smith & Wesson Model 66, 357-magnum for it and maybe threw in a little cash. It was referred to as an "assault rifle" then and in gun shops it's normally called an "AR" now. I have sold over 1,000 black rifles in my shop and nobody has ever walked in looking to buy a "modern sporting rifle," nor do any of my customers spend much time talking about taking the gun out on a hunt.

The standard AR caliber—.223 or 5.56 NATO as it's known to the purists—is a good hunting round if you are trying to kill an animal that weighs between 2 and 20 pounds, or what is usually referred to as a "varmint." Prairie-dog hunting can be fun because the dopey things just sit there next to their holes and often a whole bunch of them sit there waiting to be picked off. So it's kind of like shooting geese two or three at a time with a semi-automatic or pump shotgun, except you don't have to wade into the pond or send your bird dog off to find the kill. On the other hand, I haven't seen prairie dog listed as a "blue plate special" on many restaurant menus.

The 223 caliber is being promoted as the ideal load for hunting varmints. The truth is, however, that the less-powerful 22 magnum or 17 HMR calibers hit hard enough to be used on coyotes and a good, bolt-action Savage or Marlin rifle will outshoot any military-style gun any time. Slap a 4-power scope on a CZ 455 and the gun will shoot more accurately than you could ever shoot it out to 400 yards. And since coyotes and wolves tend to stay off in the distance when humans come around, bolt-action accuracy trumps the speed at which a semi-auto AR-style gun delivers multiple shots every single time.

Lately the word "predator" seems to be replacing "varmint" when discussions about hunting with assault-style rifles come up. This is because the word "predator" fits very nicely with the military terminology employed when talking about the AR-15. It's been a long time, however, since cattle feed lots were threatened by visits from wolves. The animal species whose existence is impacted by prohibitions against poisoning predators are elk and deer whose diminished herd size may make big-game hunting somewhat less enjoyable but doesn't really hurt the farm economy at all.

What really gives away the hypocrisy of the gun industry in trying to pretend that assault rifles are nothing more than updated versions of sporting rifles, is the extent to which the popularity of these guns has spawned a secondary product category in AR accessories whose annual sales and revenues may come close to matching the monies being coined by sale of the guns themselves. Most traditional hunting rifles required, at best, the purchase of a sling, a fixed or variable-power scope and, if one wanted to get fancy, a hard carrying case for the gun. Prices for these items range from cheap to expensive, but one can totally outfit a standard, bolt-action deer rifle with good accessories for under two hundred bucks. Moreover, if you are hunting white-tail in the Southeast, where the bulk of those critters live, most of the shots will be at 100 yards or less, which means that you don't even need a scope. I took plenty of deer in South Carolina using a 30-30 Winchester lever-action rifle with iron sights. Total cost of accessories for the gun? Ten bucks for a sling. My friend Sherrill used a piece of clothesline rope for the sling on his Winchester Model 70. Total cost for his accessories package? Zero.

Sherrill shot hundreds of deer with that gun. I'm serious—hundreds. We used to hunt bean fields in Sumter County and the farmers hated the deer because they would come out of the woods at night and eat the beans. So they would try to find a good hunter who would agree to set himself up on a regular basis to keep their fields clear. And Sherrill Smith was the best hunter you could find. He didn't even have to go around knocking on farmers' doors, they would come up to Richland County where he lived and ask him to hunt and protect their land. Our favorite field was worked by two black sharecroppers named Rabbit and Love. If they had other names it didn't matter. What *did* matter was the fact that if the deer ate their soybeans, they still had to come up with their payment or the fields would be cropped by someone else the following year.

The deal we made with them was that we were the only hunters who could go on their land and we kept half the meat. Which was something of a gentleman's agreement, if you will, because only Sherrill and I knew exactly how many deer we killed. And we killed plenty. We would walk around each field, find where most of the tracks went in and out of the woods, put up two tree stands downwind about 100 yards away, settle in sometime during the afternoon and wait for the game to show. Sometimes we hunted with 30-30 Winchesters, but if the field was too wide Sherrill would switch to a scoped 30-06 Winchester 70. I favored a scoped, 4X-power Remington 700 in 270, a slightly flatter-shooting caliber in case we had to split up and my stand was further away.

Between Sherrill and myself I think we spent maybe a thousand dollars on four rifles, two scopes and assorted this-'n-that. Today the kids spend twice that for an ArmaLite M 15 rifle, and then often trick it out with optics, custom stocks, tactical slings, bags and mats that probably add up to another two thousand or more. You can easily spend a thousand on a special laser and light combination; or maybe you'll go with a top-of-the-line night vision kit for close to three grand. Never mind that night hunting is illegal in all 50 states.

The other feature that makes assault rifles so much in demand is the degree to which, like other hobbies, the do-it-yourselfers can create or customize the product themselves. The only part of a gun that needs to be purchased through a dealer, with a consequent call to the FBI, is the part known as the receiver, which holds the gun's "action," aka the springs and parts that connect hammer to trigger and without which the firearm simply won't work. The receiver is the part of the gun which, under federal law, must also be stamped with the name of the manufacturer (or importer) and the serial number, which must be unique to that gun. But the receiver does not have to contain a single part in order to be, legally speaking, a firearm. Nor does it need to be connected to a barrel, even though without a barrel or a bolt which holds the firing pin the gun also cannot work.

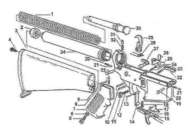

Build your own AR-15

All these parts and others can be purchased without going through a background check of any kind. There is no age requirement to buy these items; a seven-year-old can go on the internet and buy the complete parts for an AR-15 or, for that matter, any other kind of gun. He can also buy a manual that will show him, once he gets his hands on a receiver, how to completely assemble the gun. And by the way, there is no law that prevents someone for making a gun for his own use, without or without a serialized receiver or frame. You'll have to live in a state that has no state licensing requirement for gun ownership (take your pick of more than half the 50 states), but remember that the FBI NICS system records *transfers* of guns, not the existence of firearms themselves.

I'm surprised, in fact, that someone hasn't come up with the bright idea of designing handguns that could be assembled at home, although as I write this section there are reports that such guns may soon be available. Actually, you can do it quite easily with the old U.S. Army Colt pistol which, like the AR-style rifle, used to be built from the ground up as long as you got your hands on a frame. But with the increasing reliance on polymer components and MIM-technology production of parts, sooner or later the hobbyists will be able to make just about everything they want to shoot, as long as they go about it quietly and don't attempt to sell or transfer their home-made weapons to someone else.

I'm not really surprised that assault-style rifles have supplanted traditional, bolt-action or semi-automatic guns. The world changes and the market responds to change.

What I find interesting is the degree to which the industry tries to disguise the modernity and innovation of its products by trying to convince everyone, particularly the non-gun crowd, that everything's just the way it was before. But it's easy for the gun people to lie like hell about what they are really doing because the opposition, the folks who don't want guns around, are in no position to offer information or arguments that are any more grounded in facts or truth. I'll deal with all the pro and con arguments about gun violence in Chapter 4, here we'll just stick to the issue of design.

Judging from what I read and what I hear, I don't believe there is a single public figure on the gun control side of the debate who really knows the difference between an automatic and semi-automatic gun. For every NRA or NSSF misstatement about the history or use of "modern sporting rifles," there's a statement just as egregiously incorrect put out there by someone representing a group or organization that wants tighter controls on guns. When the NRA condemns the slightest attempt to impose additional gun restrictions as reflecting a secret agenda to "ban" all guns, their argument is given greater credibility when they can show that even on the most basic issues their opponents don't know what they are talking about.

Where the argument about new gun products becomes most intense, however, is in the area of kids. Until recently, children as targets of product development or gun advertising played little, if any role at all. Most surveys about gun ownership correctly pointed out that the overwhelming majority of shooters came from families where shooting or hunting was part of family life. Most people who keep guns in their home as adults grew up as kids in homes where they saw guns. And even though the argument continues to rage as to whether or not video games provoke violence in general and whether or not gun videos provoke gun violence in particular, there is scant evidence to show that kids who grew up in non-gun families but played video games then graduate to playing with real guns as adults.

Given the familial connection to gun ownership, most gun advertising that involved children depicted them involved in family shooting activities but did not in any way portray them in terms of being potential customers who might purchase guns, or influence a parental decision to own a gun. But while children aren't the direct targets of gun advertising, they can be portrayed as the future shooters who need to start learning long before they are old enough to purchase or own a gun. Many of the rifle and shotgun companies make "junior" models of their popular firearms, which usually involves cutting down the length of the stock to make the fit more comfortable for both women and children with shorter arms and smaller torsos. Recently there have also been a spate of companies that are making only junior-size rifles, often single-shot bolts, that can easily be held and fired by children under the age of ten.

Where the gun business has moved into the youth market most noticeably isn't in the sale of regular guns per se, but in what is known as "soft-air" guns that shoot gas-propelled, plastic pellets or the more traditional BBs made out of lead. Several generations of hunters first learned to shoot the Daisy Red Rider lever-action BB rifle which used to be advertised in youth magazines, chiefly *Boys' Life* scouting magazine published by and read by virtually every young Scout. My parents let me buy a Red Rider by clipping a coupon out of *Boys' Life*, putting the coupon and a ten-dollar bill into an envelope and off it went. This was 1953 or 1954 and my father, to teach me the value of money, insisted that I come up with half the cost of the gun. I was nine or ten yours' old at the time and let me tell you that earning five bucks wasn't so easy to do. So I sold greeting cards up and down the block for 50 cents a box of which the greeting card company let me keep half. I drove everyone in the neighborhood crazy, and my parents ended up buying about 10 boxes, but finally I got my gun.

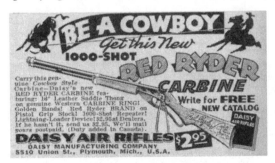

The Red Rider is still sold at Wal-Mart for forty or fifty bucks, but what the kids really like are air-soft handguns made in China which, if it wasn't for the red plastic tip at the end of the barrel, would look from a distance like the real thing. The revolution in plastics and polymers has now made it possible to turn out perfect replicas of modern guns which aim, point and shoot just like the real thing. Some of the new plastic pellet guns also have electronics that can simulate the noise of a real gun, and the most popular models are the various assault rifles, including some that fire multiple rounds each time the trigger is pulled. There are few states that impose any restrictions on purchase or use of these toys, but there are few states that impose any legal restrictions on the use of real guns by children as long as a "responsible" adult is somewhere nearby. In 2008 an eight-year-old boy shot himself to death at a public machine gun "shoot" in Massachusetts held at a local shooting club near Springfield. The boy wasn't able to control the recoil of the full-auto Uzi and a round "accidentally" tore off the top of his head. Both his father, a physician, and the show promoter, a local police chief, were indicted for manslaughter. Both got off scot-free.

Another noticeable area of growth in the shooting market involves the manufacture and sale of life-like, exploding targets which even spurt live blood when hit by a fired shell. Until ten years ago the only manufactured targets that were sold for use with guns were simply pieces of heavy paper with bulls-eyes in the middle of some concentric rings. Then targets started to be made in bright colors, as well as to look like dart boards or shooting-gallery Old Wild West scenes. The target-makers then went to another level by printing various monsters, crazy looking sub-humans and other wild creatures, as well as plastic full body torsos with macabre facial expressions right out of the Creature from the Black Lagoon.

The change in target imagery was clearly an effort to attract the video-game generation that was coming of age. Which may be good news for the ammunition manufacturers, but I'm not sure that it has resulted in the sale of new guns. It certainly hasn't convinced people who weren't raised around guns to all of a sudden become gun owners. You may recall in Chapter 1 I described a deal with the online company GroupOn to market what I called a "shooting experience" on the range in my shop. The advertising went after non-shooters who, for $25 apiece, could come to the range, shoot 50 rounds of 22LR and 9mm ammunition, get their pictures on a Facebook page and take the targets home as souvenirs. I sold over 800 sessions between September and December, 2012, a windfall that abruptly ended the day of the Sandy Hook massacre when GroupOn cancelled my action without notice.

In planning these sessions I was expecting that most of the customers would be shooters who wanted to introduce a child or a spouse to their hobby and that their experience would motivate them to buy more guns. In fact, as I mentioned earlier, I couldn't have been more mistaken. With a few exceptions, just about everyone who showed up had never previously shot or even held a real gun, but most were experienced video gamers. They had all seen hundreds, if not thousands of shootings in the movies or on television, they had shot video guns thousands of times, and now they wanted to experience the sensation of holding and shooting a real pistol in their own hands. Of the 800 or so who redeemed their coupons, I don't think 10% expressed any interest in buying or owning guns. If there has been some great awakening of interest in new gun ownership, I certainly didn't see it when these non-shooters came into my store.

The fundamental issue of guns from an economic point of view is that unless you're a hobbyist for reasons that nobody can predict or explain, owning a gun just doesn't make sense. No matter how you slice it, having a gun around the house is a risk, and as I'm going to explain in Chapter 4, the idea that a gun will make you "safe" assumes not only that you are trained to use it, but that you actually believe there's a chance you'll need to defend yourself from attack. There are all sorts of reasons why people become hobbyists and it's not unusual that hobbies change. I'm somewhat surprised, in fact, that shooting as a hobby remains as strong as it is, given how other hobbies like model railroading and model airplane building have almost disappeared. To the extent that demand for guns has been augmented of late by the shuttling back and forth of so many young men and women to battlefields in the Near East, this war cycle seems to be drawing to a close and, looking forward, the need for military manpower is increasingly going to be scaled down in favor of new technologies, such as drones and the like.

In the face of these negative trends, however, there is one aspect of the gun industry which ironically makes it somewhat profitable for those of us engaged in it, even though it's the aspect that we claim to dislike most of all. And what I'm referring to are all those messy regulations which, whether or not they have any impact on gun crime or gun safety, do have the ultimate effect of making this a rather non-competitive business in which consumer products are offered for sale. And I don't know a single person in business who is interested in competition when they are selling. Competition when you're buying? Bring it on. When you're selling? Yea, right.

This lack of competition exists at all levels of the industry. Let's start with the manufacturers. There are three companies—Glock, Smith & Wesson, Ruger—who between them manufacture and sell more than half the new handguns that hit the market each year in the United States. The top three auto makers, Toyota, Ford and GM, own about one-third of the car market. With handguns, add Taurus and Springfield Armory to the list and you're up to 70%. It may not take a lot of money to get into gun manufacturing, certainly nothing like what it takes to roll out a car, but getting into the gun market and really making an impact in terms of sales are very different things.

The same concentration exists in the other branches of the gun business, for example in long guns. For rifles it's Remington, Ruger and Savage; for shotguns it's Remington, Mossberg and Browning. In each segment three companies fill at least 60% of the market, maybe more. Ditto ammunition where Federal, Remington and Winchester may be as much as 80% of total revenues and optics in which three companies—Leupold, Nikon, Bushnell—also control most of what sells. In the last several years the startling increase in demand and the preference for black guns and their specialized accessories have probably somewhat skewed both categories and companies away from the profile described above. But even if Smith & Wesson has given up a little ground in handguns simply because nobody can meet current demand, they have regained it by moving into the assault rifle market where their AR-style rifles are doing very well.

The reason it's so hard for other companies to crack the top tier is because the major manufacturers rely for the bulk of their sales on wholesalers who are limited as to how many lines they can promote each year. Since gun manufacturers are reluctant to increase capacity even when sales are strong, you would think that with an overall increase in revenues and product margins of at least 20% that this would produce the entry of new wholesalers into the industry, just as it has produced some new manufacturers and a whole new crop of retailers. But the number of national wholesalers has remained about the same, largely because limitations on productive capacity would mean that these new wholesalers would have nothing much to sell. And while perhaps a new jobber could take advantage of the entry of new manufacturers into the market by offering them better terms and some special promotions, without the major brands to offer retailers, a new wholesaler would find it next to impossible to generate significant sales. Additionally, most of the new manufacturers, including gun makers, tend to first develop brand awareness by selling directly to the dealers or the consumers, using the money they save by cutting out the wholesale tier to cover advertising and marketing costs.

Most of the national wholesalers are also reluctant or unable to accommodate new brands because they must spend the bulk of their own promotional resources on the name brands whose sales account for the bulk of their annual revenue. So, for example, the major handgun guys usually offer their distributors two months per year of sales incentives in which the wholesale telemarketers receive cash bonuses for every unit sale and the wholesale house gets additional discounts if they hit monthly and annual sales targets. These promotions are scheduled a year in advance, the calendar fills up very quickly, and the sales force of the wholesaler isn't going to spend any time pushing a no-name product out the door when they can get a cash bonus for every Glock or Ruger that they sell.

This strategy of promoting the name brands fits perfectly into the business model of most retailers, whose livelihood is based primarily on how quickly the store inventory turns over, with most gun shops hoping to hit an inventory "turn" every 3 months. In order to move inventory that quickly, the retailer tries to limit his stock as much as possible to the brands that sell best, only ordering a new brand because a customer orders it specifically, or because the wholesaler discounts the item to get it onto the retail shelves. Either way, retail and wholesale strategies combine to keep the major manufacturers on the top of the heap, with everyone else scrambling to fill a little niche.

At the manufacturer and wholesale level, the lack of competition is due to the manner in which the distribution system tends to regulate itself. At the retail level, the lack of competition is more a function of the legal and social environment in which the industry operates at point of sale. This regulation takes three forms. First, the requirement that a background check precedes the initial sale of every single firearm means that, by definition, a lot of would-be consumers cannot enter this market. Second, while a majority of states do not have any real gun regulation at the state level, the states which do regulate firearm sales also hold the bulk of the national population. So another sizable chunk of possible consumers drop out of this particular market because they live in areas where state and local laws present barriers which they do not want to, or cannot overcome. Finally, even in areas where local laws and ordnances are lax, the number of retail locations that sell guns is often determined by the local law enforcement that may simply feel that multiple stores selling guns in their little town is too much. What this means is that the competition at the retail level is usually quite limited, if there's any competition at all. Gun shops tend to be exceedingly local in terms of the distance from which they attract their clientele, and shop owners tend to be gun hobbyists and therefore share much of their attitudes and experiences with their customers. All of which adds up to an industry that has little out in common with the competition and dynamism of most consumer sectors in the post-industrial age.

What is so fascinating about the gun business, however, is the extent to which even as limited and anti entrepreneurial as it appears to be, it continues to attract a large number of people who try to give it a shot. You can see them at local gun shows where you'll find all kinds of new-fangled products being put out for sale. There's an entire building set aside at the national dealer show, known as the SHOT show, for companies whose products may not yet even be out the door. The NRA show, in particular, seems to be a venue where new and unknown brands continue to appear.

Much of this petty entrepreneurial energy stems from the basic fact, noted earlier, that guns may be the last consumer products that are still overwhelmingly sold in independent, personally owned stores. Sure, there's a 50-50 chance that the manager of the local McDonald's may also be the owner. But owning a national franchise simply doesn't have anywhere near the degree of independence and self-reliance that comes from really owning your own store. The corporation that awarded the franchise tells you what to serve, how much to charge, which banners to display, when to open and when to close. On the other hand, I own my gun shop—lock, stock and barrel—and if I want to sit here and write this book and keep the shop closed until this chapter is complete, that's my business.

The individuality and independence of the gun retailer is what attracts so many people to create new products for a market in which the possibility for success is, at best, razor thin. The new product has to compete against an overwhelming dominance by established brands, and it has to go up against a promotion and incentive wholesale system that is almost impossible to crack. And most of all, it has to find customers in a category that hasn't really ever created new customers to any great degree. And for all those reasons, it's an industry in which the chances of being successful are exceedingly slim. But again, remember that we're talking about an industry whose products are created for hobbyists and hobbyists have a funny way of always knowing that there's just one more new product out there that other hobbyists can't wait to buy.

And now you're ready to learn the answer to the question I asked in the title to this chapter. It's an old joke in our industry so I'll repeat the question again. Want to make a million in the gun business? Start with two million.

Chapter 4

The Myth of the Armed Citizen

When I was a kid, my favorite movie was *Shane*, starring Alan Ladd. I must have seen this movie twenty times. I couldn't get over how this brave man shot and killed the bad guy played by Jack Palance, while everyone else in the town cowered or ran away. My favorite toy was a plastic silver cowboy revolver which I kept in a leather holster that tied around my waist. And every time I pulled the gun I was Alan Ladd beating Jack Palance to the draw.

That was in the mid-50's. Was it any different when Clint Eastwood began to draw down bad guys on the streets of San Francisco in the mid-70's? Eastwood was a cop and Shane was just a stranger who rode into town. But they were both armed and they both exemplified a culture that venerated the good things that could be done with a gun. Particularly a gun carried in a holster on your hip.

Clint Eastwood's 44 magnum – "Go ahead, make my day."

Unfortunately, by the 1990's it seemed that the only guys who were carrying guns on their hips were guys who were shooting other guys during robberies, gang drive-bys or screwed-up drug deals. Or at least this is what everyone believed. And the data backs this up, namely, that there was a major increase in serious felonies, particularly felonies and killings involving guns, during the early 1990's. In the late 60's and early 70's (1968 – 1972), violent crimes, according to the FBI, averaged 730,000 per year, of which 16,000 were homicides, and of those, 11,000 involved guns. Twenty years later, from 1988 to 1992, those same numbers, respectively, were 1,775,000 for violent crime, 22,000 for homicides and 16,000 for murders using guns.

In fact, it was an increase in robbery and assaults that drove the overall numbers upward, because the actual percentage of homicides of all violent crime had declined in half. But the homicide *rate* (number of homicides divided by total population) had increased by 25% over the same period. Which didn't make the whole country any more dangerous, as I will explain below. But somehow, the perception that things were getting out of control became fixed in everyone's mind.

If there was one incident that put the idea of crime on the front pages, however, it was the one involving Rodney King. He was a black construction worker who was on parole for robbery, and one night in March, 1991, he was chased, apprehended and then beaten by patrolmen from the Los Angeles police. The beating was videotaped by someone on the scene, and the tape subsequently played on a local television station. It then went "viral" worldwide (in the pre-internet sense) and inner-city violence, crime, police brutality and related stories clogged the nightly news for months to come. The case dragged on for more than a year and after four white officers were acquitted by an all-white jury in a courtroom outside of Los Angeles County, riots, arson and looting broke out in the Los Angeles ghettos, there were videos of whites being beaten and chased by blacks, the National Guard showed up, mayors of other cities toured their inner-city neighborhoods with the usual pleas for calm, and ultimately more than 50 people turned up dead.

It was in the wake of the Los Angeles riots that America became convinced that the country was no longer a lawful place. Don't get me wrong; by the numbers, crime and violence had increased over the previous several decades, mostly in the category of aggravated assaults, where the increase over twenty years was an astonishing 70 percent! And many of those assaults, even though we can't get reliable numbers, no doubt involved guns. It is also important to note that any increase in crime didn't necessarily mean that the increase was distributed evenly throughout the United States. As I am going to show below, crimes of violence, particularly gun violence, do *not* occur to the same degree in all communities. But again, bear in mind that we are dealing with perceptions, and the perceptions were that everyone was now threatened by criminals, many of whom were selling dope, and many of whom were, for the first time, heavily armed.

Some of the public concerns about armed criminals also reflected a major changes in technologies and product designs within the gun industry, because the 1980's marked the appearance of hi-capacity small arms, in particular European handguns led by Beretta, Sig-Sauer and Glock. This came about primarily because the US Army decided in the mid-1970's to replace the venerable Colt 45 1911 pistol with a 9mm, hi-capacity, double-action gun. The rationale behind the new design was to make the pistol more versatile by offering both single action (hammer manually cocked before firing) and double-action (trigger cocks gun before firing); to make it more powerful by increasing capacity from 8 to 15 rounds; and to make it more adaptable by changing calibers from 45, used only by American armed forces, to 9mm which was used by all other NATO troops.

United States gun makers had never shown much interest in pistols, largely due to the fact that police were used to carrying six-shot revolvers, a legacy, believe it or not, from old Wild West days. The major design change in American law enforcement weaponry had come in ballistics, with the 38 caliber cartridge being replaced in many departments by the much more potent 357 magnum. The problem with the 357, however, was that it was actually too potent for many law enforcement personnel, first of all because the substantial recoil meant that an officer having to fire the gun would probably only get off one well-aimed shot; and second because the bullet could penetrate then exit the human target (if it hit the target at all) and then fly through a wall and into an adjoining room and end up God knows where. Since the majority of American police patrolled urban neighborhoods, they were still largely stuck with the less-powerful 38 special round.

Beretta 92 – Official sidearm of the U.S. Army

But the bad guys weren't stuck with just anything. Once the U.S. Army decided in 1977 to adopt a U.S.-made version of the Beretta 92 pistol with a magazine capacity of 16 rounds, other hi-cap pistols from Europe, as well as guns manufactured in the United States, started to appear on the streets. Not only did these guns carry two to three times the firepower of the Smith & Wesson K-frame revolver that was being carried by just about every police department in the United States, they also used the 9mm cartridge, which was more powerful than the old 38 special but eliminated the fearsome recoil of the 357 magnum round.

There was also one other advantage that pistols had over revolvers, namely, the speed at which they could be reloaded. Not that many cops ever actually shot their guns in real-life situations, and if they did, it was rare to non-existent that a patrolman needed to fire all six rounds held by his revolver. But the speed at which an empty magazine could be dropped out of a pistol and replaced with another 15-shot mag was impressive when compared to how long it took to reload a six-shooter. Cops on duty often walked around with two gadgets known as "speedloaders," a contradiction in terms if there ever was one. These were little devices which held six cartridges and had to be placed directly over the cylinder holes, then twisted so that the new rounds would drop properly; all in all a mess. And when you finally got done, you discovered that the capacity of two speedloaders didn't even equal the capacity of one replacement pistol magazine.

The European pistols could be reloaded with another 15-16 rounds in a fraction of the time it took to reload a six-shot revolver with just another 6 shots. Finally, the pistol manufactured and imported by the Austrian gun maker Glock was built on a polymer frame which substantially reduced the weight of what had traditionally been a steel-frame gun, and was resistant to the corrosive effects of powder residue or moisture from body sweat or rain.

American gun makers were caught completely off guard by these technologies, and for the first time since the advent of the small arms industry, the United States was no longer the pacemaker in small arms design or manufacturing techniques. When the Army conducted field trials on guns submitted to replace the Colt 45, both Smith & Wesson and Colt submitted guns that didn't even survive the initial test round.

I owned the pistol that Smith & Wesson sent to the Army field trials, known as the Model 59, which the company had been making and selling without success since the mid-70's. The gun was difficult to disassemble for cleaning, was impossible to reassemble without an advanced degree in engineering, and had the nasty habit of occasionally going off by itself when the slide was dropped down after a magazine with a live round was inserted in order to reload the gun. The offering from Colt was their old 1911 gun with a 9mm barrel, a double-stack magazine and a Rube Goldberg type of trigger spring that allowed the gun to shoot double action, if and when the trigger worked at all. I didn't own one of those guns and neither did anyone else.

When the Army rejected the American-made pistols in favor of a European gun, the response by Smith & Wesson was to threaten a lawsuit which instead resulted in a second round of tests. You would have thought that before the test took place, the engineers at 2100 Roosevelt Avenue in Springfield (yes, that's the Smith & Wesson factory address) would have torn down the Beretta and the other European pistols, figured out what these guns did that the S&W gun didn't or couldn't do (basically the difference was that the European guns worked), make the necessary modifications and re-submit a new gun for the new test. You would have thought. Save that thought. They didn't make any changes at all and the American guns failed the second field tests as quickly as they had failed the first.

Once Beretta began delivery of their gun to the U.S. Army, their sales force lost no time fanning out around the country to show local police departments why they should change the guns they were carrying as well. But police departments in the big cities already knew about the advantages of these hi-cap, European guns because they were being picked up in the streets. By the early 1980's, the Smith & Wesson K-frame revolvers were being replaced in department after department by Sigs, Berettas and Glocks. Even the Massachusetts State Police, the home state of Smith & Wesson, opted to trade in their K-frame revolvers for the Sig 226. In Connecticut, where the Colt factory had produced millions of Colt 1911 pistols for armed forces here and abroad, the State Police all were armed with the Beretta Model 92 pistol, a civilian version of what the U.S. Army was now issuing the troops.

Civilian sales quickly followed the law enforcement lead. Gun shops that prided themselves on displaying and selling Smith & Wesson revolvers found that sales were boosted not by cutting revolver prices but by sticking some hi-cap pistols into the sales counter and watching their customers cart them away. The 1980's marked the first major period of handgun product innovation in the United States since Smith & Wesson's K-frame and later J-frame (a compact model) revolvers took the commercial market away from Colt after World War II. Now both S&W and Colt stood on the sidelines while the Europeans got in on the act.

Which brings us to the assault weapons ban and crime bill that was signed into law by President Clinton in 1994. This bill, as I discussed in Chapter 2, contained the ten-year ban on assault rifles and hi-cap magazines, which limited both handgun and long gun magazines to a maximum capacity of 10 rounds. Although it was called the "assault weapons" ban, it was not aimed at military-style rifles, like the AR-15 per se, but rather at high-capacity long guns and hand guns that looked more like the submachine guns that were used in street crimes, particularly crimes related to the drug trade.

On July 1, 1993, an unemployed businessman named Gian Ferri walked into a small law firm at 101 California Street in downtown San Francisco and, for reasons never figured out, methodically shot and killed nine people, including himself, and wounded six others. One of the guns he used was a Tec-9 pistol, which was a semi-automatic handgun with a 30-round magazine that looked like the sub-machine pistols carried by German SS units during World War II.

Tec-9 pistol with 30-rd. magazine.

This shooting and the public outcry that followed led directly to the assault weapons ban that was enacted the following year. Note *inter alia,* that the legislation also provided funding for more than 100,000 additional police officers which enabled the bill's supporters to pick up some votes that otherwise might have not been able to resist pressure from the NRA to defeat the measure. The bill was signed about a year after the Brady bill was passed, which marked the second legislative defeat suffered by the NRA within a twelve-month period.

In addition to outlawing the manufacture and sale of magazines that held more than 10 rounds, the law also specifically outlawed the manufacture of a number of firearms that were referred to as "assault" rifles, but were for the most part similar in design and style to the Tec-9 pictured above, including various versions of the famous Israeli machine pistol known as the Uzi. The law did not ban the manufacture or sale of European-style, hi-caliber pistols like Glock or Beretta, as long as they entered the commercial market with magazines that only held 10 rounds (handguns sold to law enforcement were exempt from the 10-shot magazine requirement). Note that the law did not ban the sale or ownership of either the assault-style guns or hi-cap magazines that were in circulation prior to the date the law took effect, and its provisions were set to expire after ten years unless they were renewed, which ultimately they were not.

I will discuss the extent to which this law may have had an impact on gun violence and homicides in Chapter 5, but for the purposes of this chapter the point is that the NRA suffered two significant defeats within less than one year. And even though stricter gun control provisions in both the Brady bill and the assault weapons ban did not survive the negotiations that eventually brought both bills to votes in the Senate and the House, the fact is that these measures represented high watermarks for advocates of gun control that would not be achieved again. The Brady bill gave the federal government the authority to deny gun ownership to certain types of individuals, whether or not the states in which these individuals resided also prohibited them from owning guns; the assault weapons ban allowed the federal government to set design standards for commercial sale of guns, again regardless of whether or not individual states went along.

This was the context in which the NRA began to promote the idea of the "armed citizen" as a defense against crime, as opposed to the government's control of guns as a response to crime. As I discussed in Chapter 2, the NRA began successfully pushing for an expansion of concealed-carry permits at the state level, a strategy that went hand-in-hand with the idea of guns being carried to protect law-abiding citizens from crime. Among other things, this strategy gave rise to the "Armed Citizen" campaign, in which NRA members were encouraged to submit stories, personal or otherwise, about men and women who resisted or overcame crimes by using or displaying a gun. The campaign first published these anecdotes in their monthly magazines, <u>American Rifleman</u> and <u>American Hunter</u>, and they are now also distributed online. It is not clear to what extent the NRA makes any effort to validate the veracity of these anecdotes, although many come from local news sources—television, radio and newspapers or other print and online outlets.

Promoting the idea of carrying guns for protection was not just coincidental with the appearance and proliferation of concealable handguns, it was a way of supporting the general shift of product categories within the manufacturing sector of the industry. In 1986, according to numbers published by the ATF, American gun makers produced 662,973 pistols and 761,414 revolvers. By 1996 pistol production increased to 987,528, while revolvers dropped to 498,944, and in 2006 pistol production was now 1,021,260 while revolvers had fallen to 385,069. In other words, over a twenty-year period, pistols moved from 46% of handgun manufacturing to 72%, a clear indication of the gun consumer's perception that self-defense with a gun was a good thing.

Which brings us to the obvious question: if everyone went out, bought a gun and stuck it in their pocket or pocketbook, would crime go down? Like just about everything else in the argument over guns, the people who say "yes" want more guns out there, and the people who say "no" want less guns out there, or maybe no guns out there. This is what I would call one of the occupational hazards of trying to be an opinion-maker or at least an opinion-presenter in this particular business: namely, everyone who is in the "talk game" about guns seems to tie what they say to what they want. I'm not surprised that the NRA publicizes research whose conclusions support their political and market agendas. What are they going to say to their members? That guns are no good?

On the other hand, I'm also not surprised that the researchers whose evidence supports calls for more gun controls are, by and large, people who would be just as happy if there were no guns. Not less guns, no guns. Why would a faculty member of a public health department advocate that the way to solve gun violence is to increase the number of guns? After all, the government lists gun control as a public health problem. The point of public health research is to find ways to mitigate health problems. If there were no guns we wouldn't have a public health issue known as gun violence, right? Want to solve the public health problem? Get rid of the guns.

So the lines in terms of what the research tells us are pretty well fixed and drawn, and later in this chapter I'm going to spend some time discussing the research on guns and violence being created from both points of view. But in the meantime, let's pause for a moment and take the NRA and pro-gun folks at their words, and assume that if you're walking down the street and a bad guy comes up to you and demands that you give him some cash, there's a better possibility that you'll hold onto your money if, instead of pulling your wallet out of your pocket, you pull out a gun. Unless, of course, the bad guy is also holding a gun. But let's assume that he's not. This is a big assumption, by the way, and it's one I'm going to bring back into the discussion when I look at the research on gun ownership and crime a little further on. But humor me for a moment.

So you've just pulled some cash out of the friendly ATM and you're about to get back into your car. It's 9 o'clock at night and you're the only one in front of the ATM. And as you turn towards the car door to fit your key into the lock (it's the wife who has the car with the electronic key that also remotely opens the door), a voice behind you says, "Hey—gimme the money you just took out of that fuckin' machine." So you turn around and two of "them" are standing there. And now what we have is the classic opening scene of the classic American one-acter known as the "mugging." One of them may be holding a knife; in the split second that you make eye contact you're shit-scared and not sure. But there are two of them. That's *why* there are two of them. To scare the shit out of you. So now what?

You can say "no" or you can say "yes." But before you decide which word you're going to use, let's detour slightly into the legal minefield known as doctrines on lethal force. Generally speaking, lethal or deadly force can only be used by non-law enforcement personnel when they believe that their life or the life of family members or others directly in their presence would otherwise be threatened by an attacker. Did you understand what you just read? I'm not sure that I understood what I just wrote, because in a situation where two or more people come into contact in a way that ends up with one of them dead or seriously wounded, things are usually not that clear. And the laws covering use of lethal force, usually grouped under the category known as justifiable homicide, vary from state to state and from jurisdiction (county, city) to jurisdiction within states.

Here's a cute little concealed gun – the S&W BGA 380.

No cop walking around with a gun anywhere in the United States receives permission to carry that weapon until he or she receives instruction in the laws covering lethal force. And not only do cops receive instruction in these laws, they must also demonstrate that they understand the laws once they go on the job. It doesn't mean that they follow proper procedures in every single case. But at least there is the recognition that if you are walking around with a piece of polymer and metal on your hip whose sole purpose is to deliver lethal force when it is drawn and used, you better know when to use it.

There is not a single state in the entire United States that requires any civilian walking around with a gun to know the laws covering legal force in the jurisdiction that gave them permission to carry that gun. Concealed-carry permits are now available for citizens in all 50 states, and no state or issuing authority within the 50 states requires any understanding or even awareness of the legal consequences of pulling that pistol out of your pocket and pulling the trigger. Want to get a driver's license? You have to pass a written test that shows whether you know that the red, six-sided sign means "stop," and the yellow triangle means "yield." Want a license to own a gun? Even in the states where you need to apply for a license before you can own a gun, and that's only 12 of the 50 states incidentally, nobody shoves an exam under your nose and then grades it to see if you achieved a passing score.

Let's get back to our little scenario in front of the ATM. The two guys have just asked you to hand over your hard-earned money. One of them is holding something in his hand which you think is a knife. They're standing five feet away and they're both bigger and tougher-looking than you. They look like they've done this before. So you quickly stammer, "okay," and stick your hand down into your pocket and you pull out—your gun! It's a little Ruger SLR 380 pistol, it fits nicely in your front pocket, holds 7 rounds and you loaded it with those Speer expanding bullets so when the 88 grains of lead hits them in the midsection it's going to make quite a hole. Or maybe you decided before you left the house that you wanted to pack a little more punch. So you grabbed your Glock Model 27, the sub-compact with the 180-grain, 40 Smith & Wesson round; the one that even if you hit them in the shoulder they're going down. No shit, they're going down.

This is what I carry – the Glock 26.

So they see the gun starting to come out of your pocket and now the "yes" and the "no" decision belongs to them. Because if they back off, the NRA's Armed Citizen website might get a good story, but the confrontation ends right then and there. You can't even pull the gun all the way out and point it at them if they're backing away because that's a crime called menacing and it's two witness statements against your one. But let's say they decide to come on anyway, figuring it's two against one. Or better yet, let's say it turns out that what you thought was a knife in the hand of Shithead Number One turns out to be a gun. Let's stop the action for a minute and introduce all the readers to Dennis Tueller, police firearm instructor *extraordinaire*.

Tueller was a firearms instructor for the Salt Lake City Police when he developed a defensive-shooting drill that is now standard issue in most police gun training. The point of the drill was to teach cops how and when to react to a deadly threat when the attacker was using something other than a gun. You see, if the guy has a gun, the moment you see it, you better draw, shout and start to bang (as in "bang-bang, you're dead"). But if he doesn't have a gun and he's standing a distance away, are you really justified in using lethal force? Maybe yes, maybe not so yes. But at least if it ends up as a "yes," you'd better be ready to bang.

Incidentally, I want to pause here for a moment and mention the ongoing "stand your ground" controversy that erupted in the wake of the Martin-Zimmerman episode in Florida. I won't bother to go into the details of the case because I'm assuming that you're not on life support, because if you are, you're probably the only living American who didn't form an opinion about this case. But "stand your ground" behavior only is connected to carrying a gun if you want to connect it to carrying a gun. In fact, the only difference between standing your ground when someone shoves you and you shove back, and standing your ground when someone shoves you and you pull out a banger is the degree of injury that will ensue if the shoving escalates to something more. Now back to Tueller.

The way the Tueller Drill works is that a police officer has to be able to draw, make ready and discharge his/her gun in the time it takes an adult male to cover seven yards. Why seven yards? Because that's the distance at which police traditionally fire their duty weapons at stationery targets on the range. Very scientific. But the point is that it takes an adult male in the age group occupied by most shitheads (16 – 24) about 1.2 seconds to cover 7 yards. So the drill requires the officer to pull, aim and hit a vital spot in 1.2 seconds or less. That's the Tueller Drill.

Now let's go back to our little scenario taking place outside the ATM. And let's pretend that the ATM is located in the lovely little town of York, PA. Why did I situate our encounter in York? Because over the last ten years, the number of concealed-carry licenses issued there each year has almost doubled, from 3,800 to 6,200, necessitating evening hours to accommodate the demand. To show you how civic-minded the local legislators are in York, two of them recently hosted a public class for anyone who was interested in applying for the license, which included discussions about concealed-carry laws and what is known in Pennsylvania as the Castle Doctrine, which is the law covering personal protection in the home. The Pennsylvania concealed-carry law doesn't require any knowledge of legalities but remember that I praised these two state legislators for their civic-mindedness.

Incidentally, the York application procedure does require applicants to answer questions about their own behavior, including the following: "Is your character and reputation such that you would be likely to act in a manner dangerous to public safety?" I'm not sure that a positive answer to that question would get someone disqualified for reasons of stupidity, but the bottom line is that the licensing procedure may include talking about this and that but it does not require any special gun training at all.

Which is hardly surprising given the fact that even in states which require some kind of training before one is given a permit to own or purchase a gun, the actual instruction really doesn't consist of any hands-on training. Most states that have a pre-licensing training requirement use an NRA course called NRA Basic Pistol, which purports to demonstrate how to hold, load, aim and fire a gun. The curriculum doesn't pay attention to the legal issues surrounding gun use, but that's not surprising since the course was developed to be used in all 50 states and gun laws obviously differ from place to place. But in my home state of Massachusetts, the course does not require a student to actually shoot a real gun.

Some training centers that offer the course use laser-equipped weapons so at least the student can see if he's even pointing the gun at the wall of the room rather than the ceiling. Other trainers use a little plastic gun with no capability of even simulating a trigger being pulled. In Florida, where as I write this chapter, George Zimmerman has been found not guilty in the shooting of Trayvon Martin, the minimum "live fire" requirement for the safety course consists of exactly one shot.

Once again let's return to our make-believe scenario in York, PA., even though, according to the NRA and the supporters of concealed carry, it's not make-believe at all. One moment you're standing next to your car fumbling for the keys. The next moment you've yanked the banger out of your pocket and if Shitheads Number One and Two don't immediately back off, you'll pop each of them one in the head and a second in the chest and down they go. You've seen it on television and in the movies hundreds of times, right?

Let's get real; here's the bottom line. Never mind the Tueller Drill. The fact is that most adult Americans can walk into a gun shop and purchase an item that delivers lethal force every time it is used without having any training in using the item at all. And yet the demand for concealed carry permits continues to grow, with police departments and issuing agencies apologizing when they fall behind. To quote the head of the Indiana State Police when, in the aftermath of Sandy Hook the deluge in concealed carry applications doubled the normal waiting time to more than three months: "We deeply regret," stated Superintendent Carter, "the inconvenience far too many Hoosiers have experienced with this process." It goes without saying that Indiana imposes no training requirements of any kind to purchase, own or carry a gun. I can't find any state which has added a training component to their gun licensing process unless it was part of the law that created the licensing process in the first place. But Texas, which used to require a training course, recently dropped it from the licensing procedures.

Here are some numbers to consider. In 2010, there were 13,164 homicides reported to the FBI from every point in the United States. Of these killings, 62%, or roughly 8,200, involved the use of a handgun. The use of handguns in violent crime deaths appears to be consistent for at least the previous ten years. Sample data from the CDC violent death database indicates that the percentage of homicides involving a gun actually increased slightly in urban areas. The next most favorite weapon, a knife, was used in 13% of all homicides. So the guy who was confronted by Shithead Numbers One and Two in front of the ATM, if they had a weapon, had a two out of three chance that what he thought was a knife was probably a gun.

But this is where our scenario begins to break down in the face of data which doesn't let us carry it forward any further. Because if the odds are much higher that the two shitheads were carrying a gun instead of a knife, the odds that our make-believe hero with the Glock or Ruger in his pants would ever be confronted by those shitheads, or any two shitheads, are astronomical. And that's because crimes involving guns, particularly crimes that end up in gun violence, don't occur in places like York, PA. When the Chief in York was asked why people were jamming into his office every night to obtain concealed carry permits, he listed as the most frequent reasons a fear of crime and a fear of terrorism, and made the point of mentioning that applications had really spiked after the bombing at the Boston marathon.

Where is all this crime taking place that's convincing everyone that they need to carry a gun? According to the FBI, most serious crime takes place where you would think it takes place—urban neighborhoods with high levels of poverty, unemployment and every other high measurement of socio-economic dislocation. In 2010, the last year for which we have solid numbers, seven states together accounted for almost 45% of all murders committed in the United States. These states were California, New York, Texas, Illinois, Florida, Michigan and Louisiana. Each of these states has at least one major metropolitan area with substantial numbers of disadvantaged families living in what we politely refer to as the "inner city." Think Los Angeles, New York City, Houston, Chicago, Jacksonville, Detroit and New Orleans. These seven metro areas and a few more within the same states accounted for 35% of all U.S. homicides, even though together these same metros are less than 5% of the entire population. Add in a couple more like Phoenix and Las Vegas and with less than 7% of the entire population, and you're over 40% of all the homicides.

Remember Indiana? This is the state where the head of the state police apologized because his agency couldn't keep up with the applications for concealed-carry permits. The homicide rate in Indiana is just a few decimal points under the national rate, but the robbery rate is 20% below the national average, and the aggravated assault rate is 26% below the national level. But let's dig a little deeper because there happens to be a city in Indiana named Indianapolis. And this city contains lots of disadvantaged people living in its inner neighborhoods. And know what happens when we look at crime data from the *rest* of Indiana? There is no crime data. The robbery rate, which registers 95.9 per 100,000 statewide (the national rate is 119.1) drops to 50.4 without Indianapolis in the mix. The aggravated assault rate, which is 186.9 for all of Indiana (U.S. rate is 252.3) drops to 113. In other words, if you live anywhere in Indiana except Indianapolis, the odds that you will be a victim of an assault are 60% less than if you live anywhere else in the United States.

I don't want to belabor this point and bore you with endless numbers, because I think you get what I'm trying to say: there's no necessary connection between the enormous spike in carry-concealed permits and the real possibility that people have to protect themselves against crime. But it's silly to assume that we do things based on some kind of rational calculation of what we are doing and what we hope will be the end result. We often act on the basis of emotion or some non-rational or non-verifiable perception. Why should the desire to protect oneself with a gun be any different? I'll tell you why. Because the decision to walk around with a gun isn't like going into a convenience store and buying a bag of potato chips, even though we know that our bodies could do without the additional calories or trans fats. It's not even the same thing as buying a pack of cigarettes. The danger created by walking around with a gun is immediate and real. If you pull it out of your pocket and put your finger on the trigger it may go off. And if it goes off someone is not only likely to be hurt, they're likely to be hurt very bad.

One more point before we rejoin our make-believe friend in front of the ATM. In the interests of full disclosure let's not forget the following: the fact that people walk around with a concealed weapons permit in their wallet doesn't mean that they are also walking around with a concealed gun. It does mean that they probably are purchasing another gun, but don't necessarily connect the dots between the latter and the former. I have yet to see one survey that actually attempted to figure out how many people are really walking around armed. In my gun shop, for example, you can't even look at a gun unless you have a state-issued gun license which, in most cases, also gives you the concealed-carry privilege. I can also tell you that very few people come into the shop with a gun on their hip. Carrying a concealed weapon around is a pain in the neck. You can't take the gun into certain locations, it's bulky and gets in the way, and so forth. When the NRA says that more armed citizens leads to less crime, they may be stretching the meaning of the word "armed" quite a bit.

Now let's go back to our gun-toting friend in front of the ATM. He's yanking his gun out of his pants and Shitheads One and Two aren't backing down. In fact they are both charging him from a distance of just a few feet. And one of them does have a knife, as it turns out. Can our hero get his gun out, level it, aim and fire in less than two seconds? Can he figure out which Shithead to shoot at first? Try this little exercise just for the hell of it. Put the book or the Kindle down and stand up facing a wall. Now visualize a spot on the wall or better yet, take a pencil and put a little mark on the wall about the height of your chest. Now stand close enough to the wall so that when you extend your arm your index finger just touches the chest-high mark that you made. Now put your hand in your pocket and when you're ready, see how long it takes to get your hand out and up and touch the exact spot on the wall. I actually perform this exercise with students who enroll in my tactical shooting class. It's a way to get them ready to try a live-fire version of the Tueller Drill. I don't think I have ever seen a student who was able to hit the mark on the wall the first or second time out in less than two seconds. Guess what? If Shithead One or Two has a knife, you're in a bad spot even with that four hundred-dollar banger that you're carrying around.

So where does the notion come from that everyone is surrounded by so much violence and crime that the only thing we can do is run out, buy a gun and carry it around? Part of that argument is supplied by the NRA, which constantly proclaims the virtues and value of the "armed citizen." This argument was first given concrete form by a pro-gun academic named Gary Kleck, who published the results of a telephone survey that was conducted in 1994 but appeared, coincidentally, in 1995 when the NRA first began ramping up its "armed citizen" campaign. Basically what Kleck claimed to have found was an enormous incidence of successful resistance against possible or actual criminal events carried out by people who either brandished or actually used a gun in self-defense. Basing his findings on telephone interviews with 222 people, he stated that as many as 2.5 million Americans had defended themselves against criminals, a number more than twenty times higher than estimates published by the Department of Justice in its annual report on crime victimizations.

THE MYTH OF THE ARMED CITIZEN

Kleck's study immediately became manna for the NRA and everyone else in the gun industry, because if what he was saying was true, it provided a reason to push for more concealed-carry permits, which would lead to more gun sales, etc. The study was initially published in a major law journal (Northwestern University's <u>Journal of Criminal Law and Criminology</u>) which meant it had to be taken seriously by other scholars, and it was, in particular by David Hemenway, a faculty member from the Harvard School of Public Health and a leading academic expert in research on consumer product safety, including such products as guns. Hemenway's critique of the Kleck survey centered both on problems of methodology (overestimations of positive desirability responses and low probability events) and problems of outcomes (extrapolating from limited samples to national populations).

Here's one example of Kleck's survey's shortcomings as mentioned by Hemenway: by estimating the number of DGU's (Defensive Gun Uses) that occur nationally based on a sample of less than 225 actual telephone interviews, Kleck's evidence effectively pointed to a total of killings and gun woundings from these episodes alone that doubled the number of gun wounds reported each year by the CDC. Since the CDC's records are based on hospital admissions, can we assume that more than one million people who sustained gunshot wounds the year of his survey went walking around *without* seeking medical care?

What one scholar later called the "DGU War" has continued between Kleck and Hemenway (plus their supporters and detractors) for twenty years. Both scholars subsequently published books that restated their positions (see my bibliography at the end) and both positions have become basic mantras for the two camps that advocate more concealed-carry permits on the one hand, and less carry-concealed on the other. If you haven't figured out which camp is which you haven't been paying much attention to what I've been saying for the past 100+ pages. The gun-carrying crew does have one point in its favor, however, which is that over the last twenty years, as concealed-carry permits have become much more popular, the amount of violent crime has also significantly decreased. I'm going to look at this issue very closely in the next chapter, so don't get lulled into thinking that a coincidence becomes an explanation as regards guns or anything else. There are, however, two fundamental issues in Kleck's survey about concealed-carry and crime that makes me tend to disbelieve all the survey results, no matter in which direction they point; namely, that many if not nearly all the alleged contacts between a criminal or a would-be criminal and the guy (or occasionally gal) with the gun go unreported to the police.

Let's return again to our friend standing next to the ATM who is in the process of pulling the Glock out of this pants. The two guys who walked up to him said, "Gimme your fuckin' money." Is that what they really said? Or did they say, "Hey, can you give us some change?" Or did they say, "How're you doin?" Let's pretend our hero is a middle-aged white guy and the two would-be muggers were BBGs (that's Big Black Guys, as some like to say in

Western Massachusetts). When was the last time that our make-believe hero was ever confronted by two black guys in the middle of the night? When was the last time our hero ever talked to two black guys anywhere at all? You think maybe if those two black guys had been two white guys that our hero would have been as scared or would have immediately assumed that he was about to get robbed?

One of the major issues that sits just off-stage in the entire gun debate is the issue of race. Why? Because you can't talk about guns without talking about crime. And you can't talk about crime without *avoiding* the issue of race. That's right: avoiding the issue. Again, please hold that thought until we get to Chapter 5. The point I'm making in this chapter is that the guy armed with the gun to protect himself against crime is usually, according to Kleck's survey, *protecting himself against a crime that hasn't yet occurred.* That's right, of the 213 complete surveys that comprised Kleck's database, virtually all of them talked about using a gun to prevent a crime that they "*thought* [my italics] might occur." And while two-thirds of the respondents said that the incident later came to the "attention" of the police, they didn't actually state that it was formally reported, nor did any of them state that in the process of reporting the incident they also reported the use of a gun.

Let me tell you a little story, and this one isn't fictional at all. I sold a nifty Smith & Wesson 9mm pistol to a guy a few years ago and about a week after he left my shop with his gun, he was in Springfield driving his small truck down State Street and he pulled up behind a car that was waiting for the stoplight to turn from red to green. As the light changed, the doors of the car opened and two BBGs got out and began walking back to his truck. He had the gun with him at the time, so he pulled it out and waved it at the BBGs, who immediately turned around, got back in their car and drove off. He hadn't gone another three blocks down State Street when his car was surrounded by police, lights flashing, fog-horn blasting, "Pull over, show us your hands, slowly get out of the car!"

It turned out that the two BBGs, after getting back in their car, jumped on their cell, dialed 911 and reported that they had been menaced by a guy with a gun. They gave a description of the vehicle and the location, but didn't describe themselves or stick around to see what then took place. In fact, the incident took place in a neighborhood that is known for street violence, so when the cops hear that someone's got a gun, they all come rushing in. My customer was detained for several hours, his story was checked again and again, and the license for the gun was also checked. Then he was let go. And the next day he came into my gun shop and told me the whole story.

Let's assume that this guy was one of the respondents called by Gary Kleck. Of course he would have answered in the affirmative when asked if he had been involved in a DGU. Of course he would have responded in the affirmative when he was asked whether his DGU resulted in a crime being stopped before it occurred. Of course he would have felt that carrying his gun around Springfield was the smart thing to do. There's only one problem: he could have been totally wrong. But if you decide to carry a gun for self-defense, there's a built-in, self-fulfilling prophecy that will lead you to assume that every time someone appears to be behaving in a way that's consistent with your notions of criminal behavior, that ultimately you'll be able to do the right thing by pulling out the gun. After all, that's why you bought the damn thing in the first place, isn't it?

The other problem with Kleck's survey, which as far as I can tell has gone unmentioned in all the critiques by Hemenway, et. al., is the basic definition of the survey as being concerned only with self-defense incidents only involving guns. Kleck states that each interview began with a few "throat-clearing" questions about "problems facing the respondent's community and crime." Now this is a dead giveaway about an inherent bias in the survey, because if you speak with someone about their "community and crime," let's be honest, you're not trying to find out when was the last time they went to Walmart. If they are a gun owner, you're telling them that they're speaking to a kindred soul. This goes back to the racial issue that we're going to talk about in Chapter 5, so hold that thought again.

The next question, according to Kleck, was whether or not the respondent had in the past five years been involved in a DGU. If the answer was "no," the interviewed ended. If the answer was in the affirmative, the questions went on. But if Kleck was really interested in establishing the true value of guns as protection against crime, the initial question should have been: "Have you been involved in a DSU," with "S" meaning "Something," as in a weapon other than a gun, or a fist, or much more likely, a voice.

Numerous studies have been published that demonstrate the fact that people who resist rather than submit to crimes end up being the victim of fewer crimes. But since we still haven't reached the point that a majority of Americans are walking around with guns, it has to be assumed (and the data from multiple studies bears this out) that the way most people resist a possible or actual crime is with something other than a gun. So if you want to make the argument that we are all safer if we all carry guns, at the very least you have to compare the results of defensive gun use to other methods of self-defense. Which is exactly what Kleck didn't do. Nor to be fair, have any of Kleck's critics raised this issue either.

The gun industry, manufacturers in particular, are aware that most of the DGUs, for which the supply of concealable guns doesn't seem close to meeting demand, involve gun owners who, let's be charitable, have absolutely no idea how to really use a gun. So to make defensive shooting easier, or at least easier to imagine, guns are increasingly equipped with lasers and other sorts of mechanical and aiming devices that take the "guess-work" out of acquiring and shooting at the target. Some of these devices, particularly lasers, were initially developed for military and law enforcement applications, in particular for units that had to secure close-quarter sites at night. Laser sighting devices are used in these situations primarily on rifles to let the shooter know the direction in which his weapon is pointed, rather than to make the actual delivery of the ordnance more accurate. The fact that most military weapons utilize a multi-shot burst shooting mechanism rather than a single shot makes the question of exact shot placement not as important as knowing the aiming point of the gun.

On the civilian side, of course, guns that deliver more than one round every time the trigger is pulled are illegal, unless one has a special license to purchase or possess what is known as a Class III gun. But such licenses are never granted for concealed-carry purposes, hence taking an aiming technology that was developed for full-automatic weapons and sticking it on a semi-automatic pistol has a lot more to do with marketing than it has to do with whether the shooter is now carrying a more accurate gun. On the other hand, the presumption is that if your gun is equipped with an aiming device like a laser, this spares you the necessity of undertaking the intensive kind of training that military and some police units undergo with weapons, whether they are outfitted with aiming technologies or not. But varying degrees of training is one thing; how about no training at all?

In Massachusetts, where I live, own a gun shop and have trained more than 2,000 people in NRA courses, including the pistol safety course required before issuance of a gun license, there is no special training needed to purchase or carry a concealed firearm for self defense. As I mentioned earlier, this is true in all 50 states. Occasionally, a local chief decides that he won't issue a concealed permit unless the applicant does something more than sit in a classroom and watch a video about safe gun techniques, if even this is required. But remember the concealed weapon course that is being given in York, PA? The most important part of the class is when the students are counseled as to proper behavior if you are questioned by law enforcement personnel about carrying a gun. The last thing anyone wants is a shoot-out between a cops and bad guy when the bad guy turns out to be a good guy with a gun. But a shoot-out between a good guy with a gun and a real bad guy? That's not so high on the list of concerns.

There are people who walk into my shop all the time and tell me they want to buy a gun for "home defense." One of these days I'll start hearing the new way in which these guns are described in NRA-endorsed instructional videos about concealed carry techniques: the new phrase is "personal-defense tool." But I haven't heard that phrase yet so let's stick with "home defense." Many of these people have never shot a handgun, some have never held a handgun. At least two people have purchased guns from me who possessed licenses to carry but were legally blind. The law in Massachusetts covering concealed permits does not list physical requirements of any kind to carry a concealed weapon. You can't drive a car in the Bay State if you can't see, but you can carry a gun.

Sometimes people come into the shop who I believe to be so woefully inadequate to own a gun, never mind carry one around, that I can't imagine how they ever were approved for a license. In selling a gun, federal and state law requires that I verify the identity of the buyer; his identity mind you, not whether he can see three feet in front of his face. When they tell me they want to own a gun for home defense, I tell them to get a dog. Or I sell them a small can of mace. I don't want them to own a gun because if they drop it and the damn thing goes off and the bullet ends up in their leg, either they'll try to sue me for selling them a damaged product (yes, I had one such suit that dragged on for more than five years), or the cops will come by and demand to know how come the gun didn't have a lock. Massachusetts is the one state in the entire United States that actually has a mandatory gun lock law, but somehow it's gotten into the noggins of some of the local police that if the gun wasn't locked up and the owner can't remember where he put the lock, it's proof that I didn't give him a lock before he left the shop.

Recall that the NRA was founded in 1871 to provide civilian firearms training. And even the NRA believes that if people are going to walk around with guns sticking out of their belts, they need proper training. Or at least that's what they used to say. The NRA has a special course, Personal Protection Outside the Home, which I am certified to teach, that covers the basics of concealed carry techniques, including types of equipment and using a gun for self-defense. The multi-day course requires live-fire exercises at distances that might typically occur during an armed confrontation, i.e., a modified version of the Tueller Drill. In order to be certified as a NRA trainer in this discipline, you also have to be certified in a series of NRA instructor pistol courses leading up to PPOH, which is considered the pinnacle of handgun instruction.

One thing about NRA training that I always admired was the degree to which every trainer has to show both experience and skills judged by the NRA to gain certification in each training discipline. And the NRA training manual insists that trainers not only behave in a completely professional manner, but are required to withhold certification from any student who does not demonstrate proper skills or demeanor in shooting. Every time I took a course as a student or as an instructor I felt that I was part of a long tradition of education and training that adequately prepared me to participate in the shooting sports. I've heard stories about poor instruction in NRA courses and you wouldn't be the first enrollee in an NRA safety course to just stand around and shoot the shit with the instructor and other students instead of learning how to shoot a gun. But I have taken more than six NRA handgun courses both as a student and at the instructor level and the guys (and gals) who teach these courses usually do a credible job.

Or they used to do a credible job. The NRA recently announced that trainers who teach basic pistol shooting courses can add an extra "module" to the course (and charge additional tuition) covering concealed carry techniques and shooting. This is an obvious and blatant effort to cash in on the concealed-carry momentum that has boosted handgun sales over the last decade. But in addition to diluting the curriculum, the standards for instructing have also been relaxed, because NRA instructors do not have to be certified in the NRA Personal Protection course; they only need to show some kind of "proof" that they have attended a commercial shooting school, like Thunder Ranch or Gunsite, in order to be certified to offer concealed-carry instruction at an NRA course.

The net effect of this new policy is that people are going to be walking around carrying loaded handguns who may have taken a minimal course taught by instructors who may or may not even possess the training credentials that the NRA used to require for teaching concealed carry. So while the NRA talks about how armed citizens make our streets and neighborhoods safer, it's pretty hard to believe that this new policy will do anything other than make people line up to buy more guns whose safe use is far from assured. On the other hand, despite what supporters of the notion of the armed citizen claim, it's not clear that the recent stampede to acquire concealed-carry privileges is in any way really related to crime or defense against crime.

Here we are back with our hero in front of the ATM. He's pulled the gun out, ready to bang away, and there's only one other little problem. He's never actually shot the gun in a situation that remotely compares to the scenario that's now being played out. Yes, he went to the range a couple of times and ran 50 or 100 rounds through the banger, but that meant aiming the gun at a stationery, paper target, not pointing it at another human being. He then took the gun home, took it apart to clean it but couldn't figure out how to put it back together. And now he's standing next to his car, the gun's in his hand and the two BBGs are closing in—maybe one has already reached out and grabbed his arm.

The possibility that our hero at the ATM will really know how to defend himself with a gun in the make-believe situation described above is about as real as the possibility that all those people who told Gary Kleck that they used a gun to frighten away a criminal actually did what they claimed to have done. So why do people actually believe that going down to the police station, filling out a form, getting printed and photographed and, if necessary, even buying a new gun, will allow them to plug the BBG who came up to them at the ATM and grabbed their arm? Because they don't believe it. They don't even think about it.

Here's the dirty little secret about the gun business that those of us who own guns understand and those who don't own guns can't even comprehend: the real reason I own those guns and the real reason I carry them around is because I *can*. I can do it as legally as Shane did it in the Old West, as legally as Dirty Harry did it when he shoved that 44 magnum into the shoulder holster under his coat. And when I hear that someone who owns a gun can do something that I haven't done, I want to do it too. Give a concealed weapons permit to a gun owner and you'd better be ready to give one to every other gun owner whom the first guy knows, because he's going to show it and brag about it every time he goes to any place and bumps into other people who own guns. Don't think for one second that the guy in York, PA who had to come back at night to apply for a permit is worried about a bomb going off in any place where he would ever go. He's standing in the hall at the police department, someone says something about a bomb, or about Boston, or about terrorism, and he repeats it because he's got to have something to say.

Last year I was standing in my shop and a guy walked in and said he wanted to buy a gun. He then added that he "knew" that if Obama wasn't re-elected that he would do "something" before Romney took over to try and get rid of all the guns. This conversation, incidentally, took place at the end of June, two days after the Supreme Court ruled in favor of Obamacare. So I said to the guy, "You know, I'm not sure that Obama's going to have that much trouble getting re-elected, given the Supreme Court's decision on his health care plan." And the guy replied, "What decision?" This guy "knew" that if Obama wasn't re-elected there was a chance he would lose all his guns. But he hadn't heard about the Court's decision on the ACA. Would this guy stand in line all night to apply for a license to carry a concealed weapon? Of course he would.

The reason that folks who buy guns for self defense don't go for real training is that the two have nothing to do with each other; getting attacked by a criminal simply isn't something that's going to happen in real life. We train to drive cars safely because we know that if we don't drive properly there's a good chance we could get killed every time we get behind the wheel of a car. But nobody really imagines that if they walk down the street without their gun that it's going to make much of a difference. Most people who aren't criminals but like to carry a gun simply enjoy the fact that they can do it; that it's there, that I can put my hand in my pocket and instead of wrapping my fingers around my key chain I can wrap my fingers around my gun. In his book *Gun Guys*, Dan Baum spends chapter after chapter trying to figure out which gun he's going to carry. Will it be a revolver? Or a pistol? Will it be new? Will it be used? After a long and agonizing search he finally settles on a Colt Detective Special, and then after hauling it around for a while discovers that it's really too heavy and too bulky to carry around every day.

With all due respect, Dan wrote a cute book but even he'll tell you that he's really not into guns. He has one carry gun? Last time I checked I have seven or eight, including a Colt revolver just like his. I also have a Glock 19 and a Glock 26, a Walther PP (*the* James Bond gun), a cute little Walther TPH, a Browning Hi-Power, a Colt 1911 and a Beretta Jetfire just to round out the current crop. And the list will no doubt change in a few months because I'm not really carrying a gun to protect myself against criminals and crime. I'm carrying a gun because I like guns.

If I were really serious about carrying a "personal defense tool," I'd practice the Tueller Drill every day or at least once a week. I'd build a little wooden barrier about the height of my car fender so I could practice ducking behind it, drawing my pistol, popping out on one side or the other and banging away. And maybe if I were really serious I'd buy one of those extra-strong tactical laser lights for a couple of hundred bucks and practice holding and shooting the gun in one hand while holding a flashlight in the other hand to illuminate the threat.

But I'm not quite that serious and neither is just about anyone else. If you ask me whether I trust the cops to defend me more than I trust myself, of course I'll tell you that I'm my own first line of defense. But there's no real connection between that statement and whether I'll actually draw my gun and fire it when the guy comes up to me as I'm standing there next to the ATM. The only time in my entire life I actually pulled a gun because I thought I was about to be attacked turned out to be a cat that had somehow gotten into the room in which I was sleeping and jumped—thump!—from the bureau down to the floor. If the NRA wants to count me as an armed citizen, let them go right ahead. I can pull my gun out and get it into a firing position as quickly as the cat can jump from the floor onto my bed. But holding the gun in my hand and pulling the trigger are two very different things. When and how does the former result in the latter? That's what the next chapter is all about.

CHAPTER 5

VIOLENCE CAN BREAK OUT ANY TIME

Before we go to the final chapter where I examine some of the more popular strategies that are being thrown around to deal with guns, I want to make one more point about gun violence with a little memoir from an earlier time. In 1969 I was employed as a caseworker for the Cook County Department of Human Services, otherwise known as the welfare department, but often referred to by the recipients as "the charity." My office was located at 1500 West Madison Street, just a few blocks away from the old Chicago Stadium where the NHL Black Hawks and the Bulls played, although I don't recall anyone going to the basketball games in those days. The stadium has now been replaced by the United Center with the statue of Michael Jordan overlooking West Madison Street, but in the days when I worked there, the neighborhood was a real shithole.

I can't describe it any other way. It was the worst, meanest and crummiest part of the inner city. And I knew every block of that neighborhood very well, because in those days the caseworkers actually went out and visited welfare recipients in their homes. So I spent a lot of time walking around the neighborhood and although I never saw another white face, I never felt worried or afraid because word had gotten around that I didn't really care whether or not someone could prove that they deserved to get the "charity." I wasn't planning to make the Department of Social Services my career, I liked hanging out and watching the kids play basketball on the concrete courts in Garfield Park, and I even enjoyed my occasional conversations with the local slumlord, an old black man named Oscar Finkley whose twenty-two-year-old son was doing time for armed robbery even though at the time of the robbery he was a paraplegic confined to a wheelchair. Don't ask how that one was pulled off.

In the interest of full disclosure, by the way, I never called Oscar Finkley a slumlord. He called *himself* a slumlord, and the reason that the plumbing never worked in the three tenements he owned was because "th'all brek it." "Th'all" being his tenants whose rent was paid each month directly by "the County," (there was only one county—Cook County) into Oscar's bank account. My job was to drop by his buildings every month or so to make sure that every apartment for which Oscar received a rent payment actually had someone living in it. Which didn't necessarily mean that it was the person for whom the County was paying the rent. I never got far enough to learn who the residents were in each unit and I didn't much care anyway. As I came walking up the street Finkley would come out of the apartment house, wave toward the building and shout, "All filled up!" That was enough for me.

So the point is that I knew the neighborhood pretty well. And one of the residents I came to know pretty well was a young black man named Fred Hampton, who was a community activist and the leader of the West Side Chapter of the Black Panther Party. I met Fred the previous year when I was at the big meeting in Lincoln Park when we planned the demonstrations that later took place at the '68 Democratic Convention. There were about 40 people at that meeting, including Dave Dellinger, Abbie Hoffman, Jerry Rubin, Bobby Seale and, as it later turned out, about 30 undercover cops. One of the black kids who showed up with Seale was Fred Hampton, and after the meeting Lee Weiner and I invited him to come and speak at a teach-in at Northwestern where Lee and I were graduate students at the time. Fred was a bright, smart and funny kid who took community organizing a lot more seriously than he took himself. So the following year when I went down to work for the county at the West Madison Street office, I made a point of meeting up with Fred again.

At that time there was a big ghetto gang operating on both the West and South Sides known as the Blackstone Rangers. The Rangers, who later changed their name to the Black Stone P. Nation, did the usual things that gangs do; i.e., dope, violence, hanging out, and so forth. They were considered one of the largest and most dangerous gangs in the ghetto world, not just in Chicago but nationwide, and even though they were headquartered on the South Side, particularly in the housing projects, they operated throughout the West Side as well.

Fred Hampton – leader of the Chicago Black Panthers

In the Fall of 1969, Chicago newspapers started reporting that there was a deal brewing between the Black Panthers and the Blackstone Nation, largely the work of Hampton, to ally the two organizations in various kinds of self-help programs. By this time, it should be added, Hoover of the FBI was referring to the Panthers as the greatest "threat" to internal security, and the State's Attorney, Ed Hanrahan, was making basically the same kinds of comments about the Panther Chapter in Chicago. If anything, his comments were even more extreme than Hoover's, if you can believe that anyone could be more extreme than Hoover.

One morning early in December I showed up at my office to be met by a group of teenage kids who insisted that I accompany them a few blocks down the street. Turned out that where they took me was the apartment in which Fred Hampton had been shot to death the night before in a pre-dawn raid that was the handiwork of a SWAT team led by the Chicago Police Department and the FBI. The room in which Hampton had been sleeping—the mattress was literally drenched in blood—was in the back of the tenement and the outer wall faced a small back yard at the end of which stood a garage.

I was told by one of the Panthers that the police had mounted a machine gun on the roof of the garage and fired at least 100 rounds through the back wall, into the room and into Fred. I could see that the wall was riddled with bullet holes; not a few holes, a whole lot of holes. And someone had pushed straws through the holes which clearly showed that the path of the bullets had come from *above* the level of the back yard. I'm no ballistics expert either then or now, but there was no question that someone had fired an automatic weapon from the back-yard garage into the house. The cops later said that they fired because someone in the house first took a shot at them. But nobody in the house opened up with a machine gun, that's for sure.

About a week later the Los Angeles Police Department staged a similar raid against the headquarters of the Black Panthers at 41st and Central in downtown Los Angeles. This was the first time that the LAPD deployed their innovative Special Weapons and Tactics squad, complete with automatic weapons, percussion grenades, helicopters and an armored car. They made a mess of it. The siege lasted for over four hours, more than 5,000 rounds were fired on both sides, and while 4 cops and 4 Panthers were wounded, nobody was killed. The end result was that the Panthers eventually were found not guilty of various assault charges and the Los Angeles SWAT team ended up being portrayed in a television series that ran for fourteen months in the mid-70's (DVD available on Amazon).

I relate this story because it's important to understand that what is violence to one person becomes the stuff of television shows to another. If I have tried to do anything in this book, it's to demonstrate that for most of us, the world in which we live is an incredibly orderly, rational and law-abiding place. Every once in a great while something dramatic or terrible occurs and it captures our attention for a moment, or a day, or a week. But unless it happens to *us*, we usually never think about it at all. In the case of gun violence, there are a lot of people who have created very nice careers, occupations and media time for themselves by telling us that this is a problem that we need to solve right now. Maybe we do, and maybe we don't.

Now let's look at some numbers. In 2011 there were 14,600 homicides, of which 11,100, or 75% were committed with a gun (I'm rounding off). The homicide rate that year per 100,000 Americans was 4.7. It turns out that the overall serious crime rate in the U.S. is not particularly greater than the serious crime rate in other advanced countries. But serious crime in the U.S. is much more violent because our homicide rate is two to ten times higher than homicide rates in other Western countries.

On the other hand, while our serious crime is much more violent than serious crime in other countries, there's also been a lot less of it lately. From 1992 until 2011, the rate of serious violent crime (homicide, rape, robbery assault) has dropped by fifty percent, and the rate of serious property crime (burglary, theft, vehicle theft) has dropped by forty percent. Serious crime has also declined in other advanced countries, but the downward trend in the United States is the most noticeable. This decline in serious crime is particularly interesting when one looks at the previous decade when, from 1982 until 1991, violent crime shot up by nearly 30%, while serious property crime rates stayed about even.

If you listen to the NRA, the decline in violent crime, particularly homicides, is due to the fact that more and more Americans are walking around carrying guns. The only problem with this picture is that it's not true because it turns that nearly 98% of the decline in homicides and overall violent crime took place before 2000, and it was after 2000 that applications for concealed-carry permits began to mount. In fact, since 2000 both the violent crime rate and the gun violence rate have begun to slowly inch upwards, a trend conveniently ignored by the "more guns, less crime" crowd.

There are a number of theories floating around, aside from the "armed citizen" theory, to explain the drop in crime over the last twenty years. Some are more plausible, some are less. For example, there's one theory out there that correlates the drop in violence with building codes that no longer allow the use of lead paint; the connection here being that lead has been shown to have some influence on anger levels in children. Want another really good one? There's the Roe v. Wade theory which states that the legalization of abortion after 1973 has resulted in less unwanted children being born who would have otherwise come of age in the 1990's. I'm sure there's also a theory out there linking declines in crime rates to global warming but I haven't found it yet despite diligent searching on the same internet where every other theory about everything can be found.

There are three theories, however, that deserve some serious comment. The first is the possible connection between crime rates and incarceration; i.e., the more people in jail, the less people out of jail who can commit crimes. And if it's not perhaps exactly a cause and effect, there's certainly a strong coincidence between these two trends. In 1986 the incarceration rate in federal and state prisons was 217 per 100,000 population. In 1996 it was 411 and jumped to over 500 in 2006, with numbers dropping slightly since that date due to the lack of space in state prison systems, most notably California.

The increase in the rate of the U.S. prison population over the last twenty years matches, inversely, the decrease in violent crime rates. For example, let's presume that the number of incarcerated prisoners in 2006 was the same as the number incarcerated in 1986 and the difference in numbers, roughly one million, was added back into the violent crime rate. This would bring the 2006 crime numbers back to where they were in 1998, which was when violent crime had dropped steeply from its highest point in the early 1990's. The problem with making an inverse correlation between crime rates and incarceration rates, however, is that since 2006 the crime rate has actually increased slightly, and so has the incarceration rate.

Second plausible theory: more cops equals less crime. There are some indications that the deployment of more police over the last twenty years certainly coincides with the decline in violence, but whether this is cause-and-effect or coincidence is not really clear. Here are some numbers. In 1992, in the middle of the great crime spike, there were approximately 800,000 sworn law enforcement officers in the United States; being "sworn" means having powers of arrest. Of this total, roughly 500,000 were in local departments (cities, towns, etc.), sheriff's departments accounted for roughly another 200,000 and the remainder were state police and special jurisdictions like state and city hospital centers, public universities, transportation facilities, and so forth. In general, most criminal policing is done by local departments because even where sheriff's deputies are the front line, most of their territories are rural which don't usually have significant crime rates anyhow. So if we are going to talk about the size of police forces relative to crime rates, we are really talking about local departments.

Here again the numbers are suggestive but certainly not conclusive. Between 1992 and 2008, the number of full-time sworn officers serving in local departments grew from 375,000 to 461,000, an increase overall of 23%, of which two-thirds occurred between 1992 and 2000. This was the same period in which violent crime declined by more than 50%. Since 2000, there has been an additional 5% growth in full-time sworn officers serving in local departments and there has also been a slight uptick in violent crime over the last twelve years.

There has been talk about new policing methods, particularly a system known as CompStat, that was first introduced in New York in 1994 and has spread to other large-city departments. Basically this system unites real-time crime data with other quality-of-life metrics to allow police commanders to both plan crime-prevention strategies and hold patrols to a more rigorous accountability for results. The implementation of CompStat in New York coincided with a significant drop in the city's violent crime rates, but the same years saw an increase in the number of street patrols by more than 30% and a parallel decline of violent crimes in cities that did not implement this system or other automated management systems. So the jury is still out.

The third theory, and perhaps the most plausible but also the most difficult to really prove with any degree of certainty, attempts to correlate the decline in gun violence, as measured by gun homicides, with advances in trauma treatment which have caused what otherwise would have been counted as homicides to be counted as assaults. Behind this theory is the fact that the last twenty years have seen advances in battlefield trauma treatment showing up in domestic medical environments, in particular the opening of regional trauma centers and much more efficient transport of trauma victims to these centers. Scholars have estimated that these new technologies may be cutting the actual number of gun homicides by as much as two-thirds what the total would be absent the existence of this new approach to trauma and gun injuries.

The problem with this analysis, unfortunately, is that if we extend the picture to cover all gun violence, not just homicides, we should expect to see an increase in gun assaults, at least enough of an increase to offset the extent to which medical intervention prevents gun wounds from becoming fatal. But the data on gun violence that includes assaults seems to indicate exactly the opposite. Over the last 20 years, in which the number of gun homicides has dropped by roughly 40%, the number of gun crimes has declined by more than 60%. If enhanced medical techniques for dealing with gun trauma could have resulted in two additional shooting victims being wounded for every victim who was killed, it strains credibility to believe that gun assaults could have declined even more quickly than gun homicides.

Finally, in addition to implausible and plausible theories, there are also what I call a number of "soft" crime-reduction theories; i.e., there's no hard data but they still make some sense. And these are theories based on experiential programs or activities that have become more common over the last twenty years. These programs include greater awareness about domestic violence, outreach to troubled families and individuals by community health and mental health organizations, anti-violence workshops as part of community-policing strategies, and a growth in child health and public health advocacy organizations.

In looking back over all the theories about why crime, violence and gun violence have decreased, there doesn't seem to be a single "silver bullet" that can be produced to explain this trend. I suspect that the answer lies in a combination of all of these factors, even though it would probably be impossible to weigh one over another in terms of effectiveness. But if the reasons why the declines violence in general and gun violence in particular remain somewhat elusive, the question that still remains to be answered is: how come gun violence in the United States is still so much higher than in other advanced countries? I think it is now clear that it's pretty difficult to make the connection between the decline in violence and the increase in the number of guns. But is there still a connection between our relatively high rate of violence and the existence of so many guns?

The notion that there's an implicit, if not explicit relationship between violence rates in the U.S. versus other countries and the free access to firearms that only we enjoy permeates the literature and public stance of every gun control advocate and advocacy organization in the United States. Take, for example, the American Academy of Pediatrics, which issued a formal policy statement on gun violence shortly after the massacre at Sandy Hook: "The absence of guns from homes and communities is the most effective measure to prevent suicide, homicide and unintentional injuries to children and adolescents." A very strong statement and one that clearly implies that access to guns should be severely limited. Here's the Brady campaign: "American children die by guns 11 times as often as children in other high-income countries." And a comment from our Number One gun-control crusader Mayor Mike Bloomberg: "The rate of firearms homicides in America is 20 times higher than it is in other economically advanced nations. We have got to change that."

So if the NRA is convinced that more guns equals less gun violence, the gun-control lobby is just as convinced that more guns equals *more* gun violence. Given the steep decline in gun violence over the last twenty years, which really occurred fifteen years ago, do the numbers really back up the gun control point of view? From an overall perspective they do, but when we drill down below the surface they really don't. Or at least they don't from the way in which the argument is usually framed. Because the truth is that, and please hold onto your hats until you finish the entire chapter, you can't really talk about gun violence unless you talk about violence in general; you can't talk about violence unless you talk about crime; and you can't talk about crime in the United States unless you talk about race. So here goes. I'm going to talk about some things that we are usually very reluctant to talk about.

Let's go back to the numbers. Bloomberg is correct when he says that the U.S. gun homicide rate is 20 times higher than other advanced countries. Our rate is 3.21 gun homicides per 100,000, Denmark is 0.27, Germany is 0.07, the UK is all the way down at 0.07, which actually makes our gun homicide rate about 45 times higher than our British cousin. But here is where we have to deal with the unmentionable. If we pull the African-American population out of the national figure, and also pull the African-American gun homicide victims out of the total number of gun homicide victims—in other words, if we calculate a gun homicide rate for everyone *except* blacks— the rate drops to 0.18 per 100,000. Since what I am now going to explain will make some people very upset, I need to explain where these numbers come from.

The author and other NRA trainers at a re-certification exercise.

In 2010 there were 11,078 gun homicides in the United States, of which 6,151 of the victims were African Americans. Which means that the total for everyone else was 4,927. This analysis, incidentally, is based on numbers published by the Department of Justice in April, 2013. According to the Bureau of the Census, the total U.S. population in 2010 was 309 million, of whom roughly 14%, or 43 million were black Americans. So let's subtract the 43 million from the 309 million. This leaves us 265 million (I'm rounding off) which gives us a gun homicide rate for the entire U.S. absent African Americans of 0.18 per hundred thousand. Isn't that what I said in the previous paragraph? Remember, don't get pissed off until you read the entire chapter. I mean it.

The calculation also gives us a gun homicide rate for African Americans of 14.3 per hundred thousand. This is higher than Mexico with their drug cartels, much higher than anywhere in East or West Europe. But we have to be very cautious at this point because what we don't know, either for African Americans or any other victim of gun violence, is the race of the person who pulled the trigger. Without knowing that information, and it simply is unavailable because the data isn't collected or counted anywhere (as far as I can tell), we cannot say for sure that the rates stated above for African-American or non-African-American homicide represent the homicide in terms of victim or homicide in terms of the person who committed the crime. We do know, however, that roughly 80% of all violent crime victims had some contact with their assailant prior to the commission of the crime itself, and we also know that more than 75% of all gun injuries occurred within the residence, or directly outside, or on an adjacent street or other location.

So, for the sake of argument and just to make sure we are not oversimplifying things, let's drop the gun homicide rate for African Americans twenty percent to 11.44 and let's increase the gun homicide rate for everyone else twenty percent to 0.21. Wow—what a difference! In comparison to other countries, no difference at all. Remember, you're not allowed to get pissed off until the chapter is done. If it were the case that looking at gun homicide figures for the entire U.S. population did not make a substantial difference with or without the data for African Americans, then the issue of race, crime and violence could be left alone. But the difference is so extreme that to ignore it would be to create not only a totally false picture of how and why gun violence occurs, but worse, to lead us down some pretty stupid directions in terms of figuring out what to do about it.

And here's the reason why we need to address the issue head on: because with all the legal barriers that have been knocked down over the last forty to fifty years, with all the opportunities for equal treatment that are now afforded minorities in general and blacks in particular, with the old stigma about interracial marriage on the wane, the fact is that most blacks in the United States still live apart from whites. For example, in 2010 there were still 30 metropolitan areas in which at least two-thirds of the black residents lived in segregated or near-segregated neighborhoods.

The 12 most segregated cities included New York, Los Angeles, Chicago, Detroit, Cleveland, Milwaukee, Cincinnati, St. Louis and Newark. We will get into the socio-economics of what the Census Bureau politely refers to as "racial dissimilarity," but I think you get the picture. The bottom line is that most African Americans in the United States still live apart from whites, and if most victims claim to have had some contact with their assailant before the crime occurred, we can safely assume that where people live is where most gun violence takes place, and in the case of African-Americans, both shooter and victims were black.

Let's drill down a little further. What follows are the homicides that have occurred in 2013 in Springfield, MA. Now, I live outside of Springfield and I travel through the city almost every day. So when I talk about Springfield, I know what I'm talking about. And by the way, Springfield made the list of one of the 30 most racially segregated cities in the United States. Anyway, here's the list:

· · · · · January 7. Victim – Norma Perez, age 57, Hispanic. Assailant – Luis Rosa, age 41, Hispanic. Stabbed in her apartment. Robbery. Then he shot himself. Assailant was victim's son.

· · · · · January 16. Victim – Jimmie Acevedo, age 42, Hispanic. Assailant – Unknown. Shot multiple times in the street two blocks from his residence.

· · · · · January 20. Victim – Reshawn Robbins, age 19, African American. Assailant – Unknown. Shot in the street.

· · · · · February 8. Victim – Julie Treadwell, age 26, African American. Assailant – Anthony Brown, age 28, African-American. Shot in her apartment. Domestic. He then committed suicide with the gun.

· · · · · February 18. Victim – Yasmin Marin, age 32, African American. Assailant – Name not released. Hit-and-run.

· · · · · April 11. Victim – Brandon Sparks, age 29, African American. Assailant – Unknown. Shot in his car.

· · · · · May 21. Victim – Fabian Pacheco, age 30, Hispanic. Assailant – Unknown. Shot in his apartment.

· · · · · May 22. Victim – Angel Lorens, age 22, Hispanic. Assailant – Unknown. Shot multiple times on the street in front of his apartment.

· · · · · June 8. Victim – Christian Graves, age 19, African American. Assailant – Unknown. Shot multiple times in street.

· · · · · June 16. Victim – John White, age 38, African American. Assailant – Unknown. Shot in street one block from his apartment during a multi-person fight.

····· July 4. Victim – Tysheanna Atkins, age 19, African American. Assailant – Terrance Brown, age 22, African American. Domestic. Shot in her apartment.

····· July 18. Victim – Unidentified male, resident of neighboring city of Holyoke. Assailant – Unknown.

Location of 2013 homicides in Springfield, 6 north of the Armory, 4 south of it.

Here's a recap. 12 murders, one vehicular homicide, another with a knife. That leaves ten shootings. Seven victims were African Americans and, like the three Hispanics, all were shot either inside, in front of, or down the block from their apartments. The locations are noted in the map above, four in the South End, four in the North End, two in what is known as Upper Hill. So far in 2013 the gun homicide rate for the city of Springfield is 7.9, three times the national rate from last year. If there are another 5 gun homicides over the remainder of the year, we end up at a gun homicide rate of 19, which puts Springfield above most large American cities with the exception of Miami and New Orleans. It also exceeds the gun homicide rate in places like Zimbabwe and Rwanda.

The city hit 19 gun homicides in 2011. That number is certainly not out of reach this year.

How did Springfield end up as such a violent place? It wasn't always that way. In fact, until the 1970's it was stable and prosperous, known primarily for the red-brick factories and machine and metalworking production that reflected the city's early entry into the industrial age thanks to the Springfield Arsenal. When the city's factories resumed peacetime production after World War II, it was the location, in addition to the Armory, of Smith & Wesson whose factory was in the South End on Stockbridge Street, the large American Bosch plant in the North End, and the Westinghouse plant at the east end of town. These companies had skilled, stable and well-paid workforces who lived in neighborhoods either adjacent or close by the factory sites themselves, and invested their earnings in home purchases and support of local businesses.

A perfect example of this lifestyle was the experience of John Garand, the Canadian-born gun inventor who designed the most famous military rifle of all time, the M-1. Described by General George Patton as "the greatest battle implement ever devised," the semi-automatic M-1 was issued to millions of American troops in both Europe and the Pacific, and replaced the venerable bolt-action Springfield rifle that had been produced at the Arsenal since World War I. Garand, his wife and daughters lived about three miles from the factory; he sometimes walked to work in the morning or walked home down Boston Road at night. When a delegation of big shots came up from Washington to present him with a medal after the War, he came downstairs for the ceremony, walked back up to his office, and stuck the medal in his desk where it was discovered by a nephew after his death.

M-1 Garand 30-06 army rifle

John Garand was typical of the skilled and loyal workers who were employed by machine and manufacturing companies all over the town. They stayed with their jobs for their entire lives, they settled in one neighborhood and that's where they raised their kids. The industrialization of America in the nineteenth and early twentieth centuries created and supported skilled, working-class and middle class communities like Springfield all over the United States.

Then things changed and in the case of Springfield, the change came abruptly in 1968. First, the government closed the Arsenal and outsourced rifle production to private manufacturers like ArmaLite and Colt. That same year the last family member to run Smith & Wesson passed away, the company was sold to a non-local investment firm, and the entire factory on downtown Stockbridge Street moved out to Indian Orchard, leaving a shuttered and abandoned structure behind. Two years later, Westinghouse shut down its large facility and by the mid-1970's, the American Bosch plant—the largest factory in Springfield—began laying off workers as its various assembly and manufacturing operations moved to cheaper areas in the South. The de-industrialization of Springfield didn't wait for the integration of the American economy into a global economy; it began to take place thirty years before the word "globalization" ever appeared.

I came up to Springfield for the first time in 1981 for a meeting at Smith & Wesson, which by then had completely moved out to its present location on Roosevelt Avenue at the eastern edge of town. But I stayed overnight in a motel in the middle of the city, which is still operating as a motel but which I suspect houses welfare families who otherwise might be in the street. I noticed in 1981 that the downtown area was beginning to look dilapidated and unkempt. When I returned for the very next time in 1993, the city had collapsed. The downtown residential neighborhoods which had provided housing for workers at American Bosch, Smith & Wesson and the many smaller machine and tools companies that sub-contracted work from the large plants were now largely comprised of burned-out or abandoned buildings. There were no restaurants or stores that remained open long beyond when the white-collar City Hall or bank employees left at 5 P.M. to drive home, and what had once been a lovely waterfront along the Connecticut River was now cut off from the city by an ugly, elevated interstate highway that made it easy to drive through Springfield without ever seeing Springfield.

Over the following twenty years since I returned to Springfield in 1993, things have changed. It's gotten worse. In 1960, when Springfield was still very much a serious manufacturing center, the city held 175,000 people. The present population is less than 150,000. In the same fifty years, the overall U.S. population has increased from 180 to 310 million; i.e., roughly 70 percent. If Springfield's growth had just kept pace with the rest of the country, the city would now have over 250,000 people. And it's not the case that the decrease in population was just because people left the inner city and moved out to the burbs. The population of Hampden County, which contains the communities around Springfield, is basically the same as it was fifty years ago.

But what is not the same are the economic and demographic conditions that define the quality of life of every community. Let's look at some numbers. Springfield is 35% white, 25% black and 50% Hispanic, almost all Puerto Rican. In 1960 the population was slightly more than 90% white. The city's median family income in 1960 was slightly higher than the national average and slightly lower than the state average. Today it's slightly more than half the state's average. Since the percentage of public employment in the state and the city of Springfield is almost the same (roughly 14 percent), the difference in median income lies in the collapse of manufacturing which today provides employment for 10% of the workforce, as opposed to more than 30% in the 1960's. Beginning to notice some patterns here? Let's continue.

The official poverty rate in Massachusetts is 7.6%. In Springfield it's 28%. The state unemployment rate is 7.8%, the rate in Springfield is 14%. Single-parent households headed by women with children under 18 is 7% of all households in the state, it's 16% of all households in Springfield. As to the value of housing, statewide more than 80% of the residential dwellings are worth $200,000 or more, in Springfield the percentage is less than 20 percent. It should be added that the overall numbers for Springfield hide significant disparities between neighborhoods. Go back to the map which shows where murders have been committed so far in 2013. The neighborhoods in which all but one of the homicides occurred have poverty rates above 40%, and unemployment rates at least twice the city-wide average. While 65% of the city's residents are high school graduates, the drop-out rate in these same neighborhoods is above 50%, and median family income is just above $20,000.

South End apartment building, typically boarded on ground floor but apartments occupied on higher floors. Apartment house in background to the right was the Stockbridge Street Smith & Wesson factory. *Photo by author.*

Springfield is a city of 150,000 people, but from the perspective of gun violence it's really three cities. The whole city exhibits a socio-economic profile that reflects a disappearance of the manufacturing base and the replacement of a skilled, employed workforce with an unskilled or semi-skilled workforce employed in low-end jobs. But within the city there are some better neighborhoods, particularly the southern and eastern parts of town like Forest Park and Sixteen Acres, which are still relatively intact, still have decent housing, and still have median family incomes that approach the levels of the state as a whole. So that's one city within the city.

Then there's the inner city, which covers most of the area within a mile or two from the river that marks Springfield's western edge. This is where virtually all of the African American population lives, along with the more disadvantaged Hispanics. And then within the inner city there's what I call an inner-inner city where the numbers on poverty, income, housing and so forth aren't just bad, they're alarmingly bad. And this is where virtually all the gun murders take place. Which means it's not even accurate to figure out a murder rate by dividing the number of murders by the population as a whole. The real gun homicide rate in Springfield should be computed based on the 10 victims divided by the population of these inner-inner city blocks. Because it's the people who live in the area where all the murders take place whose lives are impacted by this violence.

If you live two miles away across the border in Longmeadow, or even within the city in Forest Park, it really doesn't matter whether the homicide rate is 11, or 20, or 200. You're not going to see one of those bodies at all. But if you live within easy walking distance of Memorial Square in the North End, the 4 people shot so far this year adds up to a gun violence rate not of 11, but 60 per 100,000. In terms of violence, you're no longer living in the United States. You're living nowhere else. Even the South American countries with the highest gun homicide rates in the world (Venezuela, Colombia) don't go above 40 per 100,000.

Two blocks from Mason Square where 4 people have been murdered in 2013 from January to June. Note boarded up first floor apartments but occupied units above. *Photo by author.*

Notice that in just about every homicide the victim was killed either in their residence, or in front of their residence, or within a block or two of their residence. The activity of gunning someone down is about as local as you can get. The kids in those neighborhoods have to walk further to get to school, further to the community center that they visit after school, further to their Church on Sunday. But coming upon the victim of a gun homicide, just walk down the block. Maybe only half a block.

And Springfield is not exceptional in this respect, it's typical. A recent study of homicide locations in Baltimore found that the neighborhoods in which all the city's homicides occurred covered less than 1% of the city's total land space. If you live in Baltimore outside this 1% of the city's total area, you never see anyone who's been killed with a gun, or killed with any other type of weapon. In Washington, D.C. the homicides were somewhat more distributed throughout the city between 2004 and 2006, but if you lived between Connecticut Avenue and the Potomac River, an area comprising one-fifth of the city's total real estate and containing just about all the white residents, you also wouldn't ever see a single homicide.

And there's one other point that needs to be made about gun homicides. Let's not forget that the gun control crowd isn't just saying that we have too many homicides. What they really mean is that we have too many homicides because we have too many guns. So let's assume for the next couple of paragraphs that the number of gun homicides correlates directly with access to guns. The problem for my gun control friends is that this argument cuts both ways.

For example, the per capita rate of gun ownership in the United States is 94 per 100,000. In Italy and Denmark the per capita ownership rate is 12; i.e., 8 times lower than our rate. So let's multiply the current rate of gun homicides in Italy and Denmark by 8. Guess what? Their 'adjusted' gun homicide rate exceeds our rate by almost half. In other words, we have lots of guns floating around, but comparatively speaking, we also have a very *non-violent* population. Sorry, but when the NRA talks about all those law-abiding gun owners out there, they know what they're talking about.

So this is where the analysis about gun violence stands so far. It's black, it's concentrated both geographically and economically, and where you find the innermost part of the inner city is where it takes place. But hold on. Don't put me down as just another race-monger about crime. Because what I have analyzed to this point only gives us a profile for *one-third* of the gun violence that occurs in the United States. The remaining two-thirds involve suicides, and the profile for that type of gun violence is much different. The basic difference is in the race of the victim, because in the case of homicides, we seem to see blacks shooting other blacks. In the case of suicide, it's whites who turn the gun on themselves. A different kind of violence, but still violence committed with a gun.

As opposed to gun homicides, which have declined by more than 40% over the last twenty years, suicides began to drop slightly beginning in 1990, declining by about 15% until 2000, and then moving slowly upwards again until the rate per 100,000 in 2010 was just slightly less than what was recorded twenty years earlier. While guns are used in 75 to 80 percent of all homicides, self-inflicted gun wounds have accounted for roughly half of all suicides during this same time-period. And guns are a very efficient way to commit suicide, because almost everyone who tries to end their life with a gun succeeds, whereas the next favorite method—hanging—works about

65% of the time and taking too many pills leads to death in less than 10% of all known occurrences.

Which is the real problem in talking about suicide regardless of the method used, namely, that since it's not a crime, the data that's available for understanding the problem isn't very good. Suicide, after all, is usually an intensely personal affair, as are most extreme types of mental illness. For a country that is obsessed with health, it's physical health that garners all the attention and on which we spend so much public and private monies. The whole question of mental health is at best occasionally discussed, at worst usually ignored. And since suicides are not considered crimes, coroners and medical examiners are not under the kind of public scrutiny when filing a death certificate on suicide that would be true if they were filing a death certificate for, let's say, a homicide. So this part of the chapter is unfortunately going to be based on much less rigorous data than we can use when talking about gun deaths that are also crimes. Nevertheless, certain basic trends do emerge.

First, our suicide rate per 100,000 is high, but not that high. We rank right around the rates for Denmark, England, Canada and other advanced countries whose gun homicide rate is ten to twenty times lower than ours. We are also far below countries with extremely high rates, like Lithuania, Kazakhstan and Belarus, which average in the mid-20s per 100,000 while our rate is 12, and everyone falls far below the extraordinary 108 rate of Greenland, whose number simply cannot be explained with reference to any of the standard reasons (depression, alcoholism, etc.) that promote suicide everywhere else.

Another way in which our suicide rate is fairly typical is the gender division of the victims. Recently, a spurt in overall suicides has drawn attention to the fact that males outnumber female victims by at least four to one (which is also the gender ratio in gun homicides and homicides in general, by the way). But again this profile is fairly typical of other countries—in France and England the gap is slightly less, Poland somewhat more, but everyone basically falls within the same four-to-one ratio.

When it comes to the racial composition of suicides, however, the profile changes. White male and female rates are more than four times the rates for male and female blacks. This is true in all three age groups for which the CDC classifies suicide data: ages 10–24, 25–65 and 65 and above. Interestingly, the only age group in which white and black suicide rates are somewhat comparable is ages 10-24, where the white rate per 100,000 is 13 and the black rate is 8. When we move to the 25-65 cohort, the gap is much more extreme: white males have a rate of 30(!), while black male suicide per 100,000 is just over 12. Go to the 65-plus age group and the gap becomes even wider, with the white rate at 32 and the black rate at just 10. The overall suicide rate for whites in the United States is 16, the rate for blacks is 6. So just as black homicide rates push our overall homicide rate to the highest of all advanced countries, the low black suicide rate pulls our overall suicide rate down to somewhere in the middle. If we talk about homicide as a black problem, we have to talk about suicide as white problem.

This is the reason that I asked you earlier not to yell and scream when I brought race into the issue of violence. Because death that is caused by conscious behavior *that otherwise would not be considered "normal" behavior* cannot be arbitrarily separated into "good" and "bad" categories. As a society we have decided that it's a crime when one person takes another person's life, but it's just an unfortunate event when someone takes their own life. But is the impact of the victim's demise substantially different on family and friends? Of course it isn't. There's the same loss of income, the same disruption to family, the same disappearance of a loved one, and so forth. Don't get me wrong; I'm not saying we should criminalize suicide or de-criminalize homicide. What I am saying is that both are types of violence, particularly when committed with guns.

Overall, roughly 54% of all suicides in the United States are committed with guns. This is the highest use of guns in suicides in any advanced country, although as I mentioned earlier, the U.S. is not a particularly suicide-prone nation. What's interesting, however, when we break down the use of guns for suicides by race, we discover that blacks and whites use guns to exactly the same extent: 48 percent white to 50 percent black in the 10-24 age group, 50-50 for ages 25-65, and 72 to 72 among black and white suicides above the age of 65. What we can therefore say is that while the differential in homicide rates are driven by the use of guns by blacks, the differential in suicide rates is not a function of suicidal whites using guns; it's a function of the low suicide rates among blacks.

The distinctiveness of white suicide can also be seen when we look at its geographic distribution. Note this: There are eight western states—Colorado, Arizona, Idaho, Montana, Nevada, New Mexico, Utah, Wyoming—who between them contain 7% of the U.S. population and account for 11% of all suicides. Each of these states has a suicide rate at least 20% higher than the national rate. In some states like Montana, Wyoming and New Mexico it's almost double the national rate. The suicide rate in the western states would drive the national rate higher were it not for the fact that these states contain so few people. And despite what many people believe, suicide in the western states isn't pushed up by Native Americans, because overall their suicide rate is lower than the national rate.

To sum up the data on suicide: it's a white male problem. And even though teen suicides have been increasing lately, that behavior is tied to male teens who happen to be white. Which brings us to the issue of suicide and guns. No other country has the prevalence of firearm use for suicides as does the United States. The western states, for example, where the suicide rate is twice the national average, all have ownership and household possession of guns above 50 percent. Some experts have suggested that if guns weren't so available our suicide rate would go down. But the argument, while suggestive, is based more on coincidence than cause and effect. There are other states, particularly in the Southeast, that have as high a rate of gun ownership as the western states but have suicide rates within the national average. And many European countries that have higher suicide rates than the U.S. have a much lower rate of gun ownership.

Can guns be viewed as the drivers of suicide among whites the way they appear to be drivers of homicides among blacks? Notwithstanding the lack of concrete data that definitively supports either argument, I happen to believe that guns do play a role in elevating levels of violence in both crime and suicide, not so much because of the role played by the gun, but by the role played by anger which ultimately results in reaching for a gun. When we consider the factors that lead to violence, one factor and one factor alone stands out: we are looking at anger that is out of control. Anger is perhaps the most powerful human emotion and it often serves a valuable purpose both in terms of protecting oneself from harm, or what one expert calls a "natural, adaptive response to threats." But using anger constructively is one thing, turning it inwardly or outwardly in a destructive way is quite another.

Pediatricians and other early childhood experts have long been aware of the fact that social dynamics and behavior observed and experienced by children at an early age can have a profound impact on their ability to manage and control anger as they pass through childhood, the teen years and beyond. Young children who are subject to verbal or physical abuse, or see it happening around them, begin to exhibit difficulty in accepting or dealing with frustrations and disappointments before they begin school, and their response to discipline or demands to modify behavior often make them "problems" whose presence in the classroom and other social environments is not welcomed or desired. "The sins of the father will be visited upon the sons until the seventh generation," says the Bible, and this is certainly the case when children are exposed to physical, mental or substance abuse in their home or neighborhood settings.

In neighborhoods where incomes are marginal at best, home life is chaotic, everything appears to be left to chance, and the possibility that children will grow up without the ability to constructively manage anger must be immense. So it's not surprising that the anger so easily turns to violence. And here is the dirty little secret that I have waited until exactly this page to let escape: when it comes to expressing violence, there's nothing, just nothing like a gun. There's no other object on this earth that does it as well, as efficiently, as easily and, I hate to say it, as dramatically.

Want to feel powerful enough to overcome those fears of insecurity that arose when the man you thought was your father stopped coming home? A gun. Want to believe that nobody's going to slap your face again the way your face got slapped every time you cried? A gun. Want to know you can earn the money you need by selling more dope than the kid selling across the street? A gun. Want to make sure that girl you've been seeing won't go out with someone else when you're back is turned? A gun. For those of us who live a normal, disciplined, productive life, it's difficult to imagine that a gun can solve those kinds of problems. But it's difficult to imagine that we would even face such problems or couldn't deal with them without letting our anger get out of control.

But don't assume that anger management failure and the consequent reliance on a gun is a function only of the inner-inner city life. Because for every ghetto black who exhibits anger by pulling the trigger of a gun, there are two white guys out there, mostly middle class, who also have a problem managing anger and turn the anger inward on themselves. One lost a job and all of a sudden can't find money to pay the bills. Another discovered that his devoted wife has been having a hot and heavy affair, and her lover is another woman so what does that say about *him*? And then there's the guy who just can't stop drinking and even the pills don't work anymore. So he went to the doctor two weeks ago and was told to go see a therapist but nobody can give him an appointment for the next three months. Gun violence isn't about crime and it's not about race. It's about violence. Violence with a gun.

It is the impulsive use of a gun to exhibit out-of-control anger, regardless of whether this anger is expressed outward or turned inwardly, that makes attacks against physicians by the NRA so destructive and so absurd. In the case of children who show anger management issues at pre-school age, it's the pediatrician who usually spots the problem. Why shouldn't the doctor then inquire about guns? Get over the 2nd Amendment nonsense folks; children with extreme anger problems pose a greater risk to safety if they get their hands on a gun.

As for behavior that leads to suicides, evidence indicates that a majority of suicide victims actually met with a medical professional two weeks or less before they ended their lives. Some of these victims might have been able to hide their symptoms, but most went to see the physician or therapist because they needed help. Should caregivers in these situations be prohibited from asking about guns? The NRA says that such questions should be criminalized because they threaten the constitutional "right" of the gun owner to own a gun. That's not just absurd, it's an insult to every American who depends on medical professionals for their health and well-being. And if this statement turns me into an "enemy" of the 2nd Amendment, so be it. You can go on my blog, mikethegunguy.com and tell me how much you hate my point of view.

I am 68 years old, and the only time in my entire life that I ever felt my life was in any way threatened by a gun was when I mistakenly strayed across the border at night from Morocco to Algeria, and somewhere on a back road near Sabra was stopped by an Algerian border patrol who thought that maybe I was driving at such a high speed because I had stolen the car. It wasn't a very pleasant experience to stand at the side of a dirt road in the middle of nowhere with an Algerian gendarme who didn't speak a fucking word of French poking a sub-machine pistol into my ribs.

The title of this chapter was actually what a young black, gang-banger wannabe said to me when I asked him why he wanted to carry a gun. His answer was, "violence can break out any time." As far as I knew, he didn't live remotely close to any neighborhood where a murder had ever occurred. And in fact his parents owned their own home in an integrated, suburban neighborhood not far from the hospital where his father was employed as a physician's assistant and his mother was a cook. He ended up maybe quitting high school, worked menial jobs a bit here and there, was arrested for attempted auto theft on more than one occasion and, thankfully, disappeared from my family's life before things got any worse. In theory he was right; violence can break out any time. In practice, it doesn't break out if you're educated enough to read and understand this book. You may spend your life talking or researching about violence, but there's a pretty good chance that you'll never actually see it. Think about that.

CHAPTER 6

DO WE KNOW WHAT WE KNOW?

I'll begin this chapter with just a bit more data to make sure that I've covered all of gun violence. In 2012 there were 700 deaths from gunshots that were ruled as "accidents;" i.e., unintentional injuries. To put this into perspective, more than 3,000 people died from recreational (non-boating) drownings that year, of which probably one-quarter died in backyard pools, both in-ground and inflatable. When was the last time that a backyard drowning made the national news? But when a five-year old in New Jersey picked up a loaded gun during a backyard barbecue and drilled his three-year old sister *while the parents and other adults were standing around*, it got headlines all over the place.

Sorry, but I happen to side with the NRA on this one. Sometimes we pay a price for being an idiot or just being careless. With all the safe designs, seat belts, air bags and so forth, human error is still the leading cause of traffic deaths in the United States. This is probably the case with every other category of unintentional injury. Why should we single out guns? I'll tell you why at the end of the chapter. In the meantime, let's single them out and look at what everyone wants to do about them.

I'll start with the gun control crowd, first things first. In my thirty-five years in the gun business I have never encountered anyone who sincerely believed in gun control and happened to own guns. Every once in a while when the gun debate gets particularly shrill or venomous you'll find a gun owner or two, usually of my generation or vintage, who gets embarrassed by the pro-gun rhetoric of Ted Nugent and quietly allows that "maybe we need to control things a little more." Or they will tell you that the problem is that there are too many "nuts" out there; as if uttering that phrase gets the issue off the table. But they don't really mean it. Believe me, they're much more concerned about the price of gasoline than whether or not the government expands background checks to cover private sales.

On the other hand, or on the other side, I also don't know anyone who sincerely believes in gun control and actually owns a gun. Some of them may feel obliged to say something positive about the 2nd Amendment, but it's like an atheist who tells you that he supports the religious freedom guarantees in the 1st. He has to say that in order to be seen as being reasonable, but the truth is he couldn't really care. After all, the Constitution doesn't really say that it will protect his right to *not* believe in God, so why should he care if it protects the rights of those who do? So when the NRA says that the gun control crowd really wants to get rid of all guns, to a greater or lesser extent they're correct. But it's not so much an active desire to go out there and effectively confiscate all that metal junk which motivates the gun control folks, it's more a passive feeling that there's no good reason to have the damn things around.

Which is both the strength and the weakness of the anti-gun crusade. It's their strength because when they get vociferous and very public about controlling guns, they'll be matched or outshouted by the other side, but no matter how off-the-mark their proposals really are, at least they don't have to worry about dissenting voices from within their own ranks. At the same time, since anti-gun sentiment in this country is hardly a hot-button issue, the gun control crusaders also run out of public support before anything substantive can ever get done. Want a perfect example of this yang and yang? Let's start with Mike Bloomberg and his Mayors Against Illegal Guns.

Bloomberg started his anti-gun crusade in 2006 when he mounted an operation against alleged "straw" sales by sending undercover operatives into gun shops which had previously sold guns that ultimately were used (and then confiscated) in New York City crimes. The operation was run out of Bloomberg's office, it didn't involve the ATF, nor were local law enforcement organizations contacted in the jurisdictions where Bloomberg's representatives purchased or tried to purchase guns. On May 15, 2006, Bloomberg announced that New York City was suing 15 gun dealers for illegal sales of guns to Bloomberg's operatives who went into these shops and were able to transact "straw sales." He also posted a video on the internet that ostensibly shows two investigators first being refused the purchase of a gun and then being allowed to purchase; the video being referred to as an example of a legal and then illegal gun transaction.

I have watched this video multiple times. But before I tell you my reaction to it, let me first tell you the following: I like Bloomberg very much. I thought he did a wonderful job of re-energizing the city after 9-11 and I think his efforts to deal with public health issues by encouraging walking and prohibiting or limiting trans fats and caloric drinks are exemplary. But when it comes to guns, he's just not telling the truth. Or to be more precise, what he claims to be true may have little to do with the truth. At least not the truths about guns that I have learned over the last thirty-five years. Here's a couple of examples:

Bloomberg claims that there's been a steep decline in serious crime in New York because of his tough policy on guns. In fact, the drop in New York's serious crime is slightly less than the decline that's happened nationwide, even in areas where there have been no changes in gun laws or even where gun laws have become less strict. There's also serious talk in New York that the Mayor's crime numbers aren't shall we say, as exact as he claims. And finally, even many of Bloomberg's supporters admit that the drop in crime is largely due to a continuation of computer-aided community policing developed during Rudy Giuliani's tenure, combined with very aggressive stop-and-frisk activities that are probably unconstitutional and will eventually be outlawed.

But back to the so-called "straw" sale. The video allegedly shows a man and woman standing in front of a counter negotiating gun sales in two shops. In both shops the man engages the dealer in a brief conversation about a gun and then when the dealer brings out paperwork to be filled out, the man tells the dealer that "she" is going to sign for the gun. The dealer in the first shop balks at this, claims that he doesn't want to sell the gun because the man was the one who asked all the questions and the woman didn't seem interested in the transaction at all. Midway through the exchange the dealer asks the man if he is legally able to buy a gun and the man says "yes." But the dealer continues to insist that he doesn't want to sell the gun because he's not sure that the gun isn't for the man.

So two people come up to the counter, and when asked a direct question by the dealer about whether the man can buy a gun, the undercover operative lies to the dealer who, for all we know, isn't actually a dealer at all. Or maybe the dealer heard that people were going around pretending to be customers when, in fact, they were posing as customers in order to see whether transactions were being conducted according to Hoyle. But as far as I could see, if that dealer had consummated the sale, there was nothing that occurred that could have made the sale illegal. In the second part of the video, a man and woman walk into another shop and the same rigmarole proceeds again. The guy asks all the questions, the girl fills out the form, the dealer packs up the gun and some ammunition and out the door they go.

Guess what? Both sales were legal. And I'm going to spend some detailed time and analysis on this issue because there has probably been more talk about background checks and straw sales in Congress this year than on the deficit, immigration, national security or anything else. Here's how the system works: after a gun is selected, the customer fills out the ATF Form 4473. There is nothing in the law that requires anyone purchasing a gun to talk to the dealer about *anything* before the purchase takes place. There is also nothing in the law that prohibits anyone who accompanies a purchaser into a gun shop from talking to the dealer about the gun that is being purchased, including holding it, taking it apart, or doing anything else with it whether the actual purchaser touches the gun or not.

Form 4473 is what the dealer uses to call the FBI and conduct a background check. The purchaser must give his/her personal identifiers (name, address, age, physical characteristics, race), and then answer a series of questions to establish that they meet federal legal requirements to allow the purchase to take place; i.e., not being a felon, a fugitive, an unlawful narcotic user, etc. But before answering those questions, there's one additional question that needs a response: *Are you the actual transferee/buyer of the firearm(s) listed on this form?* The answer to this question is the issue on which the entire debate over straw sales rests. Because if you say "no," the sale stops at that point. If you say "yes," the dealer then calls the FBI to make sure that what's in their database agrees with what you have said about your legal and/or criminal background. Later in this chapter I am going to get into the whole issue of why the government doesn't go after people who give false

215

information on this form. In the meantime, let's stick with the transaction itself.

So the customer has filled out the form and signs his/her name which follows an affidavit in which the purchaser, by signing the form, "understands" that he/she could be found guilty of a felony if anything they said on the previous page turns out not to be true. Now the dealer takes the form and before contacting the FBI, fills out another section that verifies the identity of the customer. This generally consists of a driver's license or other government-issued ID, but it must at the very least contain a picture, an address and a date of birth. Once the identity of the buyer has been established and the FBI allows the transaction to proceed, the gun can be given to the buyer, or handed to anyone else standing with the buyer because the gun has now legally been transferred.

Here's the important text taken directly from the instructions for the 4473 form itself: *Any seller who transfers a firearm to any person they know or <u>have reasonable cause to believe</u> [my underline] is prohibited from receiving or possessing a firearm violates the law, even if the seller has complied with the background check requirements of the Brady law.* Want to try and define "reasonable cause?" I can tell you that in my shop, reasonable cause for denying a purchase would not be based on who talked to me about the gun, particularly if the transaction involved a male-female couple in which the man talked to me about the gun while the woman wandered around and tried on one of our cute Browning hats. When my wife and I walk into the Men's Department at JC Penney's because I need some shirts, it's my wife who picks them out, sometimes engages the clerk in conversation, and pays for the clothing if I'm wandering around another part of the store. Then we go into Dick's Sporting Goods and I buy the golf equipment while she looks at the clothes. Get it?

Incidentally, don't think for one second that the FBI is all that worried about whether someone really needs to pass a background check in order to get a gun. Last year these two goombahs walked into my shop, Louie and Allie, who wanted to transfer ownership of a bunch of handguns from one to the other. Turned out that Louie had lost his gun license for doing something stupid or other, so the police picked up his guns, sent them over to me for safe-keeping, and then in walk the two guys so that I can transfer the guns from me to Allie.

So Allie fills out the 4473 while Louie stands there cursing the police, his ex-wife and everyone else, and I make the call to the FBI and they tell me that they can't approve the transaction because they need more time to check things out. They don't deny the transaction, they delay it for 3 business days, and if I don't hear from them within 3 business days I can, at my own discretion, proceed with the transaction on Day 4. Think this is unusual? It happens all the time. Some buyers are delayed because the FBI database isn't complete and an additional inquiry into state records has to be performed; other times the purchaser has a personal identifier that is so close to someone else that the FBI examiner wants to make sure that the gun isn't going to the wrong person. I'm never told why any particular transaction is delayed but it happens perhaps 5 percent of the time and, more often than not, I don't hear back from the FBI within the required 3 days.

I didn't particularly like the two goombahs and I figured that if one was an actual shithead the other probably was a shithead too. Shitheadedness tends to run together, and the fact that these two shitheads were also brothers led me to believe that the goose was also the gander. So I kept putting off the transfer because every time I called the FBI they told me that while the 3 days had long ago elapsed and they couldn't stop the guns from being released, according to them the official status was still a "delay."

Meanwhile the two brothers keep calling and in addition to cursing the cops, the ex-wife and everyone in general, they also start cursing me. One day I get a call from an agent in the local ATF office who tells me that the brothers have contacted him and are really pissed off and demand that I transfer the guns. When I respond by telling him that I'm not sure I want to release the guns to such a shithead, his answer was, "Well, you do what you have to do. It's in your hands."

Fuck it, the next day I released the guns. If Allie the shithead had taken the guns out of my shop, given them back to Louie the shithead and Louie had gone home and banged (as in shot, not screwed) his ex-wife with one of the guns, I can guarantee you that the headline would have read: Gun Dealer Releases Guns to Man Who Then Kills Wife. The point is that when it comes to making decisions about whether someone should be able to buy a gun, there's the FBI, the ATF and then the dealer—me. The FBI and the ATF have all the data, all the resources, all the expertise. Know what I have? I have Allie and Louie standing in front of my counter telling me that I "better give 'em those fuckin' guns." And Bloomberg's going to send some undercover whatever-they-ares into my shop to see whether I'm making sure that the person who talks to me about the gun is the person who's buying the gun? No wonder that none of the lawsuits that Bloomberg initiated against all those rogue dealers ever got through court.

Mayor Michael Bloomberg announcing something about guns.

Despite the fact that none of the gun-trafficking dealers whom Bloomberg sued were found either negligent or guilty in court, this didn't prevent the good crusader from following up on this project with a second salvo in 2011, this one aimed at the internet and the alleged black market of anonymous and illegal gun sales being conducted online. Dubbed "Point, Click, Fire," this scheme used operatives from the international security firm, Kroll, who went online and allegedly bought guns from private sellers who were told by the undercover agent that the gun was being sold to someone who could "probably" not pass a background check. The conversations were taped and, in at least five instances, the transactions were actually completed face-to-face with an exchange of cash for guns. Like the gun shop stings, these transactions, including tapes of the telephone conversations and photos of the guns, were posted on the Mayor's website and sent to media outlets worldwide.

In the same way that I watched the gun shop sale video multiple times, so I also listened to the audio of the internet sale multiple times and it's interesting theater, but it's more make-believe than real. To begin, you can always take an extreme case and use it to explain anything. And if the audience you're trying to convince doesn't know much more about the issue than you do, it's not difficult to prove your case—at least to them. But Bloomberg didn't prove it to me and here's why. The actual exchange between buyer and seller was as follows:

Buyer: You're not one of those licensed guys, right?
Seller: No, no, no.
Buyer: No background check?
Seller: No, I just take cash, and there you go. [Laughs]
Buyer: Alright, no background checks—that's good 'cuz I probably couldn't pass one of those things.

First, telling a guy in casual conversation who's going to sell you a gun that you "probably" couldn't pass a background check is like me telling my wife that all I had for lunch was a piece of lettuce and a boiled egg. If I wanted to get her into a serious conversation about why I never seem to lose weight, I'd sit her down and say something to the effect of, "Why do I keep eating two doughnuts every afternoon with my coffee break?" The guy who's selling the gun just wants to sell the gun. And he doesn't really care whether the buyer can pass a background check, it's just another bit of conversation.

But here's the real bottom line. The guy who listed that gun for sale on the website *armslist.com*, which features and promotes private sales, also probably listed it on every other website that features gun sales because gun selling websites, as opposed to eBay, don't charge for listings until a gun is actually sold. In fact I have sold more than 600 guns on the largest and most active website, *GunBroker.com*, and although I list myself as a dealer and require all guns to be transferred from my dealer's license to another dealer's license, you would think that at some point I would have received at least one call from a buyer who wanted to fulfill the transaction off-line. It's never happened.

I'm not saying there aren't bad people out there. I'm not saying that every gun dealer in the United States is a saint. And I'm certainly not saying that every single person who has held a gun in his hands is nothing other than a law-abiding sportsman; eleven thousand gun homicides and 1.5 million non-fatal gun victimizations each year proves that statement wrong. But what I am saying is that the fact that some undercover agents, or actors, or whatever they were, held brief conversations with guys who then couldn't wait to get rid of a gun and get their hands on some cash proves only that the guy who sold the gun needed some cash. It doesn't prove anything about the motives of the seller or even if he really knew that he was engaging in a transaction that was against the law.

If Bloomberg was convinced that the acquisition of those "illegal" guns involved the active complicity or at least the passive acquiescence of the seller, why didn't he report those sellers to the police of the jurisdiction in which the transaction took place? After all, it's against the law to knowingly transfer a gun to someone who cannot meet federal and local requirements for gun ownership, and the law applies to everyone, not just to dealers. So if the seller continued the transaction after he was "told" that he was selling his gun to a prohibited party, didn't Bloomberg and his people have the moral, if not the legal responsibility to turn the guy in? They had the gun, they had pictures and audio, and they certainly could have marked the cash. I'll tell you why they didn't go to the cops; for the same reason they didn't go to the cops after visiting all those so-called rogue dealers in their shops. They didn't have a case. They had theater.

Just to make sure we don't leave any stone unturned, the NRA and its supporters have their own, favorite little issue about dealer-customer relations that they trot out at every turn to show how "serious" they are about wanting to keep us safe. Their big deal is to insist that the ATF become more aggressive in going after gun buyers who fail the NICS check because, after all, the 4473 tells every buyer that lying on the form is a felony and can result in a federal prosecution.

At some point the news got around that less than 1% of all the names of people who failed the background checks were followed up by ATF. And this statistic became *excuso numero uno* for why background checks didn't need to be extended to private sales because, after all, the FBI and the ATF weren't even doing a good job going after the miscreants who shouldn't have filled out the form in the first place. This argument is pure crap and any politician who raised it as a rationale for voting against background checks should be ashamed of him(or her)self for saying something this stupid in a public debate. Going after someone for "lying" on a 4473 is about as realistic a legal strategy for curbing gun violence as arresting someone for counterfeiting who uses a Canadian coin in a vending machine.

But back to Mike Bloomberg. When the debate over a new gun law erupted after Sandy Hook, the Mayor took center stage. First he convened a symposium on gun violence at the Center for Gun Policy and Research, which is a program at the Johns Hopkins School of Public Health endowed by—you guessed it—Bloomberg himself. The contributions to the symposium consisted for the most part of previously published research, sometimes updated to account for new data, sometimes not. But by and large the contributions were academic arguments that bolstered Bloomberg's gun control strategy and were, in the main, what the gun control crowd and their allies in the Democratic Party brought to the Senate floor in April, 2013. It's therefore worthwhile to examine these proposals in some detail, because they are the counterparts to the NRA "Armed Citizen" strategy for expanding gun ownership that we analyzed in Chapter 4.

Like the Allied plan to invade Nazi Germany after the sweep across France in 1944, Bloomberg's strategy consists of three main thrusts. First, keep guns out of the wrong hands by expanding background checks to cover all private sales. Second, toughen gun trafficking laws so that guns purchased or stolen in one state don't wind up somewhere else. Third, limit the availability of military-style ("assault") weapons and bring back the ban on hi-cap mags. How do these proposals really stack up?

Bloomberg and everyone else in the gun control lobby claim that 40% of all gun sales in 2012 took place without background checks. Actually, they claim that 40% of all gun sales take place without background checks every year, a statement that is mantra in the gun control community, even used on multiple occasions by the President himself. There's only one small problem. The number is made up of such whole cloth that I'm almost embarrassed to explain where it comes from—but I will.

In 1994, during the debate over the Brady law, the Police Foundation and the Department of Justice did a telephone survey of gun owners to determine, among other things, not only how many guns existed in the United States, but the means by which they had been acquired. To the question about whether the gun was acquired from a licensed dealer and therefore subject to some sort of legal regulation, sixty percent stated that they acquired the gun from someone whom they believed to be a "licensed dealer." So you know what? If you subtract 60 from 100, you get 40. And believe it or not, this is where the figure of 40 percent of gun transactions that take place without a background check comes from. That's right. A telephone survey conducted almost twenty years ago and based on an inferential mathematical analysis of limited data.

How limited was the data? You may recall that back in Chapter 4 I analyzed in some detail a survey conducted around the same time by Gary Kleck that purported to prove that citizens with arms had prevented more than two million crimes each year. And how many people were interviewed by Kleck and his survey team? A grand total of 225. And how many people would you guess were interviewed by the survey team that found out that 40% of all gun owners had acquired their guns without background checks? A grand total of 248. And to leave you a little more bewildered about this survey, note that it was conducted in 1994. Which means that not a single gun transaction that was conducted in a dealer's shop was actually verified by a background check. Why? Because in 1994 when this survey was conducted *there were no instant background checks*. The NICS system didn't even start operating until 1995 and wasn't fully operational until 1999.

So the total and complete data cited again and again in an entire national debate between gun control advocates on the one side and gun freedom advocates on the other, gets down to two surveys conducted twenty years ago using responses that totaled less than 500 people in both surveys, none of whom would have been able to answer the questions with any degree of certainty or reality anyhow. Is it any wonder that there were no WMD's in Iraq?

Just for the sake of argument, however, since we don't have any other data, let's stick with the 40% non-compliant gun transactions and see where it takes us. I promise you that it takes us to a very interesting state of affairs. According to the FBI, there were just under 20 million NICS checks performed in 2012. Since NICS inquiries can involve the transfer of multiple guns, let's round the number up to 20 million as to the number of guns that were actually transferred with a background check. Now we don't yet have data on the number of guns manufactured in 2012, but thanks to the ATF we do know the total that were imported, which is roughly 3.5 million. And since this number has been pretty steady the last couple of years, as has the number of guns manufactured (because the factories are running at full capacity thanks to the ineptness of the Romney campaign), we can use manufacturing numbers from 2011 with good certainty and we wind up with a total of roughly 8 million new guns entering the market in 2012. We can also assume that for every new gun that entered the market a new gun was sold because dealers had no trouble turning over their inventory in 2012.

Now here's where things get a little dicey. Because remember that I said that NICS calls don't distinguish between new and used guns. But in my shop, which is pretty typical of most medium-sized shops, of every 10 guns I sell, roughly 6 are new and 4 are used. So if we had 8 million NICS checks for new guns, there were probably another 3 or 4 million checks for used guns. This leaves us with 8 million NICS queries that simply can't be accounted for by new or used guns sold out of dealer inventories. So let's add another 2 million, and I'm being generous, believe me, for internet sales in which the gun transaction is between two individuals but the seller sends the gun to a dealer designated by the buyer.

Guess what? We're still left with 6 million calls to NICS that can only be the result of private individuals walking into a gun shop and asking the dealer to do a background check on their behalf. And before you raise the old gun show bugaboo, remember that all licensed dealers must conduct background checks on all guns they sell, regardless of whether the sale takes place in their shop, at a gun show, or anywhere else. Sorry Mike, Barack and the latest gun control hero Joe Manchin, the numbers of NICS checks that cannot be explained by dealer or internet sales going through dealers are between 30 and 40 percent of all NICS calls. Gee, that's funny. I thought that 40% of all gun transactions didn't involve background checks. And by the way, let's not forget one more little point: even though Bloomberg may want to believe that internet sales creates yet another way for people to avoid background checks and get their hands on illegal guns, it's actually the reverse. Because since most internet sales do, in fact, go through dealers, this means that a lot of guns that otherwise might have gone directly from seller to buyer in private sales now actually come back into the regulated market, not the other way around.

As for the question of chasing gun traffickers more aggressively, the Mayor seems to be confusing the shipment of guns from one point to another for illegal sale in the latter and the so-called "straw sales" that his undercover operatives allegedly transacted in 2006. Let's assume for a moment that the straw sale which his people video-taped and put on the internet was, in fact, an illegal sale. Is there any reason to suppose that the fact that someone is unable to own a gun means that they will commit a crime once they get their hands on one? In my state, Massachusetts, the law requires that you cannot hold a gun license and own or purchase guns if you have been convicted of DUI. I suppose the rationale here is that people who drink and drive are dangerous, hence owning a firearm makes them more dangerous. But guys come into my shop all the time and tell me that they can't buy a regular gun because of a DUI. They still want to go hunting, so instead they purchase a black powder gun for which no gun license is required. Are these guys going to go out and commit a crime with a gun?

I'm not trying to defend the indefensible. If I were to pull 30 pistols out of my display case, stuff them into the trunk of my car, drive three hours down to New York and then find a bigger idiot than myself who would take them all off my hands for cash, I'm guilty of gun trafficking. But when a guy and his wife come into my shop and she buys the gun because she has a permit and he lost his for one reason or another—I didn't just have a visit from Bonnie and Clyde. Taking that gun to Worcester and re-selling it in the ghetto is the furthest thing from their mind. They wouldn't know where the ghetto was located in Worcester. They wouldn't even know how to get to Worcester.

Finally, back to the old assault weapons thing again. It's true that Adam Lanza used an AR-15 at Sandy Hook; the shooter in Aurora also carried a semi-automatic rifle with a hi-cap mag. But do you know how many New York City residents were shot in 2012 with rifles, any kind of rifle? I guarantee you it was less than the fingers on one hand. How do I know that? Because in all of New York State the number of homicides committed with any kind of long gun was under ten.

I'm probably the only gun dealer in the United States who believes that there may be a connection between magazine capacity and violent crime rates, if only because the steep drop in violent crime and gun homicides that took place between 1994 and 2000 coincided with the first half of the ten-year assault weapons ban that included a ban on the manufacture and sale of new, hi-cap magazines. On the other hand, this was also the time that many of the most violent cities were also able to deploy additional police officers due to the law enforcement funding provisions contained in the same legislation.

The NRA and its allies are correct in pointing out that gun violence of all kinds almost entirely involves handguns, with rifles and shotguns accounting for less than 5% of all fatal and non-fatal gun crimes. It should be pointed out, incidentally, that the 1994 ban on high-capacity magazines did not just apply to assault rifle magazines, it also covered pistol magazines for brands like Glock, Smith & Wesson, Sig and other manufacturers. I have never understood why hi-cap mags and assault weapons always appear as inseparable items on the agenda of Bloomberg and the other gun control advocates, particularly since the reasons for banning the former have little, if anything to do with limiting access to the latter. But as I think you understand by now, there's a lot about the gun debate on both sides that makes little sense to me.

What should make more sense, however, was the decision by the President, in January 2013, to resume CDC-sponsored research on gun violence, or at least define the topics that should be investigated even if funding for CDC-sponsored projects remained unavailable. Twenty years earlier, in 1993, the *New England Journal of Medicine* published an article based on CDC-sponsored research that made the case for home ownership of guns being linked to increased homicides. The article appeared during the run-up to the 1994 gun debate and from that time onwards, physicians were in the sights of the NRA. By 1996, the NRA succeeded in cutting funding for gun research out of the CDC budget, and while they were not successful in closing down the remarkable gun homicide data collection contained in the National Violent Death Reporting System, they were able to stymie a plan to enlarge this database to include data from all 50 states (current data is available for only 18 states).

In April, following Obama's January Executive Memorandum calling for renewed research, a national meeting of experts convened in Washington to establish priorities and topics for renewed gun research. The report that they issued in July, 2013 established six basic areas of research: (1) types and characteristics of gun violence, (2) risk and protective strategies, (3) prevention interventions and strategies, (4) impact of gun safety technologies, and (5) video games and other media. The report also summarized what was known to date about each research area, cited relevant bibliography and publications, and listed specific questions that might form the basis of various research projects in each of the six areas. Research on these topics, according to the experts, "will improve current knowledge of the causes of firearm violence, the interventions that prevent firearm violence, and strategies to minimize the public health burden of firearm violence."

So here's my thoughts on this report, and I may be the only person outside of the report's authors who has read every word of it, including most of the bibliographical sources and previous research on which it is based. I'm not saying that to pat myself on the back. I'm saying it because it's a very long and very wordy document followed by 235 references to books, articles and reports in such mainstream publications as *Personality and Social Psychology Bulletin* and *Journal of Urban Health*, among others. With that said, here's my summary (with comments of course) on the six research areas that the experts believe we need to undertake in order to figure out what to do about guns:

1. <u>Characteristics of Gun Violence</u>. This section begins with the usual canto about our high homicide rates, then understates the percentage of handguns used in violent crime, notes that suicides are more

frequent than homicides, and adds that "rural areas tend to have higher rates of firearm suicides than urban areas, while urban areas have higher rates of firearm homicides." Further on, the experts also note that "the firearm-related homicide rate was significantly higher for blacks than Asian/Pacific Islanders, whites and American Indian/Alaskan Natives."

As for further research, the report calls for more information on how guns get into the wrong hands (none of the Bloomberg theatrical productions are mentioned anywhere in the document), why people acquire guns in the first place, and what factors may be similar and different when guns are used in non-self-inflicted (homicide) as opposed to self-inflicted (suicide) ways. Both in this research area and others, the report is careful to underscore the importance of "interdisciplinary partnerships among academics, practitioners, and community members," although at no point are these three groups identified further in terms of which types of individuals would belong to which group. I'm wondering, for example, whether the practitioners of non-self-inflicted gun violence would include the gun bangers, whereas the victims would probably be included in the community group, right? Let's continue summarizing the report.

2. <u>Risk and Protective Strategies</u>. The report identifies four levels of risk factors that can affect the rate of violence: society-level, community-level, situational-

level and individual-level. What this jargon means in English is that if a country is poor, or a community in a country is poor, or a family in a community in a country is poor, or an individual in a family in a community in a country is poor, the risk of violence increases. Get it? Since gun violence is a specific form of violence, the trick here is to figure out how each of these risk factors is connected to guns.

In particular, the experts would like research to focus on how children get their hands on guns, whether locking guns away makes it more difficult to use them in suicide attempts, and how to identify geographic "hot spots" where gun violence frequently occurs. All three of these issues need to be considered within the context of private gun ownership and storage, because according to the report, such research would "be invaluable to individuals wanting to make an *informed decision* [my italics] about the benefits and risks of keeping a gun in their home."

I must confess a certain bias here about how people who earn their livings by conducting research view the results of what they learn. It's one thing to sit in a laboratory and figure out how to change the chemical composition of lipstick so that your employer, let's say Revlon, can market a new lipstick that stays bright and shiny on someone's face for longer than the competitive brand. That kind of research has a direct and immediate benefit that can easily be explained to anyone who might want to use the product. But when it comes to research about the way we behave, when the research is based on the assumption that if we change our behavior something "good" will happen, I remain somewhat skeptical about any resultant cause and effect.

I'm going to end this book in a few pages with a story about something very stupid I did with a gun many years ago. For the moment, let's just consider the following question: do we really need to learn that guns are dangerous things? Please hold the answer to that question for just a few pages more.

3. Prevention interventions and strategies. When asked to come up with a model for dealing with gun violence, public health experts, including the experts who wrote this report, invariably cite the significant drop in highway fatalities as an example of how changes in design coupled with education and enforcement brought about a significant decline in highway deaths. The report states, "During the past 20 years, significant declines in death and injury from automobile crashes, fires and drowning have been achieved through comprehensive prevention strategies that recognize the characteristics of the agent, the victim, and the physical and social environment in which the injury occurred. A similar public health framework may be particularly effective in the case of gun violence..."

I think we can move right past the drowning and fire issues because roughly 3,500 Americans lose their lives in each of those injury categories every year, which is about 10% the number who die from car wrecks or gunshot wounds. But as to highway fatalities, with all due respect to the public health intervention model, the fatality rate in the U.S. has dropped roughly one-third (15.57 in 1993 to 10.84 in 2012) in the last twenty years, while the overall gun violence rate has dropped by 25 percent and the gun homicide rate has declined by more than 40 percent. Too bad the experts are still searching for a comprehensive strategy to curb gun violence because if we had one, it could also be used to reduce highway fatalities.

4. Impact of Gun Safety Technologies. Here again the experts appear to be borrowing a chapter from the auto safety playbook, because there does appear to be a clear connection between safe car design and the reduction in highway fatalities, particularly since the use of the most effective safety device—seat belts—is also backed up by aggressive enforcement. In the case of guns, however, the problem is that no "safe gun" technology has yet been developed, even at the prototype stage, that can allow the user to actually discharge the firearm without first manually disengaging the safety device. For all the talk about biometric systems that would automatically recognize a specific fingerprint, or magnetic encoding that would automatically lock or unlock the firing mechanism with the presence of a magnet encoder,

there has yet to be a market developed for such products due to cost and a lack of reliability.

The real problem with safe gun technology, however, like all consumer safety products, is that if they are not installed in the product at the point of manufacture, most consumers can't be bothered or believe they can't afford to purchase or install a safety device. The fact that federal law prohibits the Consumer Product Safety Commission from regulating guns makes the idea of any industry adoption of these technologies a dead letter, even if their adoption might result in a few less dead human beings. I don't know of any consumer product industry that ever freely adopted safety measures without the intervention or threat of intervention by public authorities.

It should also be added that guns as they are currently engineered (and have always been engineered, for that matter) don't readily reflect the increased reliance on new technologies, particularly digital technologies, that have spurred innovation in just about every other consumer industry. There's something of a cultural time-lag in gun ownership and I'm not sure that the current interest in guns will be sustained as the next generation comes of age and possibly sees this product category as outmoded and under-designed.

5. Video Games and Other Media. Don't think that only ivory-tower academics are concerned about the possible link between violence in the media and gun

violence. One of America's foremost authorities on gun violence, Wayne LaPierre, who denies its existence on a daily basis, was quick to blame "media conglomerates" for the carnage that took place at Sandy Hook. He added that these companies "compete with one another to shock, violate and offend every standard of civilized society by bringing an ever-more-toxic mix of reckless behavior into our homes every day."

The authors of our report agree that there has been substantial and, for the most part, inconclusive research on the links between media violence and violence in behavior. But they go on to call for additional research into the possible connection between violent media and gun violence in particular. So in writing this section of the book I consulted with a pediatrician who specializes in adolescent medicine and asked her whether she believed that kids who spent 4 to 5 hours each day playing video games (the most recent study from the Kaiser Foundation actually puts the average daily video gaming much higher) were more likely to graduate from shooting games to real guns. And here was her exact response: "I don't care about that. What concerns me and other doctors is that the kids sit on their rear ends all day long, eat potato chips and drink caloric soda and get fat as hell. They'll die from diabetes a lot sooner than they'll die from a gunshot wound."

MICHAEL R. WEISSER

That may be true. Childhood diabetes will eventually kill a lot more children than will be killed with guns. But that doesn't mean we should simply step away from the problem of gun violence and decide there's nothing to do. What I have been trying to do throughout this book, however, is to explain some of the real issues that need to be understood in order to respond to the problem of gun violence with strategies that might actually work. After all, if we don't understand what gun violence is, how and when it happens, and who is involved, how can we ever hope to even have a realistic discussion about the problem, never mind respond to it in realistic and effective ways? The point of this book is to try and explain what we really know about gun violence and what we don't know. If I've managed to give you some new ideas in both respects, then this book has accomplished a very great deal.

In sum, here's what we know and what we don't know. We know that gun violence is a very efficient way to engage in violent behavior, and violent behavior is anger that is out of control. It appears to be the case that African-American males express this anger outwardly, while white males appear to turn it inwards on themselves. What accounts for this difference? We don't know.

We do know that guns are lethal and they are the only consumer product whose sole purpose—design and function—is to kill. If you bring a gun into your home you have created a risk that doesn't exist with any other consumer item. Now it's true that more children die in backyard swimming pools each year than from gunshot wounds. But lots of kids fall into pools and are pulled out

238

before they drown. The young boy who puts a loaded gun against his sister's head and pulls the trigger won't be able to jump in the pool and save her life. Is there a way of designing or handling guns that will mitigate this risk? We don't know.

We have two sides in the gun debate who know how to talk to their own constituencies but don't have a clue about what to say to the other side. So we know and we don't know. But if you really want to know what I know about guns, here's a little story I've been saving for the end of the book. Ready?

Picture 1978. It's about eleven at night. I'm sitting in the living room of my ranch house in a quiet residential neighborhood in Columbia, South Carolina, re-assembling a Colt 45. Wife and kids are asleep, and I'm just sitting, cleaning and having some fun with my gun. I stand up with the gun in my hand, pop a mag into the grip, rack the slide and damn if the thing don't go off. Boom! Right through the front door, shatters the glass in the storm door, flies off don't-know-where. Hot*damn*. Nobody in the house wakes up, neighbors don't turn on any lights. Done is done.

My house on Mockingbird Lane with front door repaired.

Next morning I notice Mr. and Mrs. Beckham, a lovely elderly couple whose house faced mine from across the street, standing in front of their home talking to their next-door neighbors, Mr. and Mrs. Todd. Now I've known these people for a few years and we're good friends, but this here's the South so I always call them Mister and Miz, which is the way it is. Next thing I know my three-year old Amanda goes scampering out the front door and runs across the street, because she knows that Miz Beckham's going to give her a cookie and ask her if she's been a "good little dahlin." But Miz Beckham didn't ask her that question this morning. To the chuckles of her husband and the neighbors she done say to Amanda, "Go back over yonder and ask your Daddy what time he shot out that front door." And Amanda scooted right back and asked. So I stepped outside, waved to the Beckhams and the Todds, and they waved back. Then we all had a good laugh. Know what? The day started off just fine.

* * *

NOTES ON SOURCES AND FURTHER READING

I'm sure that nobody was upset when they started reading this book and didn't find any footnotes. But this isn't a doctoral dissertation and it's not meant for the academic audience, although I am a former academic and, in fact did write a doctoral dissertation. On the other hand, every single bit of data referred to in the book can easily be found, and here is where:

1. FBI – Uniform Crime Reports and NICS reports.
2. U.S. Census, in particular the neighborhood survey.
3. CDC, mostly the WISQARS Leading Causes of Death Database and the National Violent Death Reporting System.
4. Department of Justice, in particular the Bureau of Justice Statistics, various reports and data collections.
5. ATF – mostly the data on manufacturing and imports, along with several of their occasional studies and reports.

I also used some state level data that is found in relevant state government departments. I did not use data from any of the advocacy organizations (Brady Campaign, Violence Policy Center, etc.) because as far as I can tell, this data all comes from the public information cited above anyway. Additionally, much of the information about gun violence is based on crime data that is usually 2-3 years behind in terms of publication date, even though it is often referred to as being current data. The plethora of web-based gun violence organizations that have been put up since Sandy Hook post endless commentaries about this killing and that killing, but they are just aggregating daily search results from Google and elsewhere.

As for additional reading, I cite some relevant and/or interesting books in alphabetical order. If you read them or even skim them you can sound pretty knowledgeable the next time you find yourself at a cocktail party with nothing better to talk about.

Dan Baum, <u>Gun Guys, A Road Trip</u> (New York, 2013). Reads a little like a screenplay for a Michael Moore movie about guns, except that Michael already made a movie about guns. Fun to read although maybe a little less kvetching about how difficult it was to choose a carry weapon. Baum answers emails so he may not be a gun guy but he's a good guy.

Joan Burbick, <u>Gun Show Nation</u> (New York, 1906). Brilliant, inside look at the gun culture from someone who knows how to walk into a room and figure out what's going on.

Tom Diaz, <u>The Last Gun</u> (New York, 2013). Right now the *non plus ultra* contribution from the gun control crowd, complete with a laundry-list of "solutions" which won't keep the NRA leadership up at night.

David Hemenway, <u>Private Guns, Public Health</u> (Ann Arbor, 2004). Directs the Injury Control Research Center at Harvard's School of Public Health and is probably most responsible for defining gun violence within a public health context. The Center's effort to develop a "safe storage" program for suicide risks is exemplary.

Gary Kleck, <u>Targeting Guns: Firearms and their Control</u> (Hawthorne, 1997). Updated version of a book initially published in 1991. Kleck's research is condemned by the gun control crowd and beloved by the NRA—take your pick. But he also answers emails so he's a good guy too.

Adam Winkler, <u>Gunfight</u> (New York, 2011). An objective analysis of the 2008 SCOTUS decision even though it's not that easy to write a whole book about one Supreme Court case, particularly since we're not talking about *Brown v. Board of Education* or *Gideon*.

For entertainment:

Glenn Beck, <u>Control, Exposing the Truth About Guns</u> (New York, 2013). To Glenn's credit, he knows his audience.

And the best of all:

Jimmy Breslin, <u>The Good Rat</u> (New York, 2008). Recall I said that you can't talk about guns without talking about crime. Thanks to the lovely Starbucks café in my local Barnes & Noble, I read at least one true crime book a week. This one I bought, took home and read it again. It's the best.

Acknowledgements and Complaints

Over the years, whether they knew it or not, there were people who helped me learn about the gun business. And I'm not sure I remember everyone but here's some names that deserve to be mentioned in no particular order: Carl Carson, Clyde Gates, Jon Galef, Lou Imperato, Joe DeSaye, Salvador Colom, Dennis Healey, John Reiger, Don Blanshaft, Sherrill Smith and Ben DeMain.

I want to send a special thanks to David Hemenway who read the entire manuscript with sensibility and care.

And a pat on the back to Garen Wintemute, MD, who combines an acute sense of medical reality with an appreciation for the gun thing.

As I mentioned in the section on further reading, this book is not aimed at an academic or scholarly audience, but it is based on a rigorous analysis of public data, nearly all of which is available from the CDC or the DOJ. On the other hand, there are a few obsessive-compulsive readers out there who actually like footnotes. If I receive enough requests, I'll do a "scholarly" edition complete with notes, etc. Just go to www.mikethegunguy.com and let me know. You can also use the same blog to list any complaints, comments or thoughts you have about the book or any subjects herein. I'll try to answer every communication.